THE CREATIVE
Hot & Spicy
COOKBOOK

WHITECAP BOOKS

Watercolor illustrations by Sally Damant

Designed by Stonecastle Graphics

Edited by Jillian Stewart

4525
This edition published in 1997 by Whitecap Books Ltd., 351 Lynn Avenue
North Vancouver. B.C., Canada V7J 2C4
© 1997 CLB International, Godalming, Surrey, UK
Printed in Singapore
ISBN 1-55110-554-3

Contents

Introduction

Spices have been used in cooking for many thousands of years, but it is only relatively recently that cooks have begun to experiment with the many and varied cuisines that feature spices at their heart. From China, through Asia, the Middle East and North Africa to Mexico, spices are the essential ingredient in numerous authentic and exotic dishes.

The reasons for the rise in popularity of hot and spicy food are numerous and contentious – some say it is the natural outcome of the increase in travel to exotic locations, while others claim it is a result of a failure to realize the potential of our own home-grown cuisine. Whatever the reasons, hot and spicy food – whether it is an authentic recipe from overseas or an innovative fusion recipe from one of our own top chefs – is now a permanent feature of restaurants and kitchens across the country.

Basically spices are the dried parts – the seeds, pods, bark, and roots – of certain aromatic plants that usually flourish in hot countries. Flavorings from the stems and leaves of the plant are usually classified as herbs. Coriander is a good example of how different parts of a plant are divided; coriander seeds are classed as a spice, whereas the leaves and stems are a popular herb. The huge number of spices available makes it possible to create an endless variety of flavors from different combinations of ingredients. Indian cuisine, in particular, is renowned for the number of ingredients it often requires, while the cuisine of Mexico relies on a more limited, though nonetheless tasty, combination of flavors. It is precisely the way in which locally available spices and ingredients are combined, that creates the wide variety of distinctive hot and spicy dishes from around the world.

The fact that so many spices are now readily and cheaply available is something our ancestors would have found incredible. In ancient times spices were a rare and valuable commodity in the West – largely because of the difficulty and expense involved in their shipment – and as such, were the province of the wealthy. Today, modern methods of production and transportation mean that spices, like many other exotic ingredients, are readily available and affordable far from their country of origin. This does not mean, however, that finding a good supply of the ingredients you will need for these recipes is as easy as walking into your local supermarket. The key to producing good hot and spicy dishes is to use the freshest ingredients. Unfortunately, many supermarkets do not have a particularly high turnover of spices and many will have been been stored for months, by which time they will have lost much of their flavor. With this in mind it is always advisable to buy whole spices and grind them yourself or buy ready-ground spices in small quantities from a supplier with a quick turnover.

Obviously it is not just spices that lend dishes their heat, fresh ingredients such as chilies and fresh ginger root are just as important. Like spices, fresh ingredients should be bought in small quantities and not

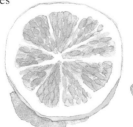

stored for any length of time. Fresh ginger root, once unheard of in many parts of the States, is now more readily available, and should be bought in very small quantities as it deteriorates rapidly. Advice on buying chilies is probably unnecessary as thousands of books have been written devoted to the subject of chilies. Simply buy them as fresh as possible and don't store them for any length of time and you shouldn't go wrong, or why not try growing your own. Everyone varies in how powerful they like their chilies so the rule is to follow what your taste buds dictate. Do be careful, however, about drastically altering the amount of chilies in a recipe as this can affect the balance of flavors, as well as the fieriness of the end result.

As you would expect, the range of hot and spicy recipes is enormous, so we've gathered together what we hope is a representation of some of the best recipes from around the world – Mexican, Indian, Chinese, and Thai, for instance – and mixed them with some home-grown specialties to enable cooks of all abilities to explore the delights of hot and spicy cooking.

Appetizers

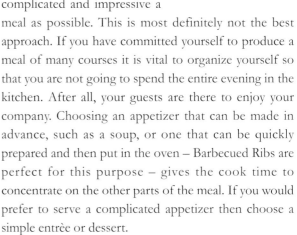

Choosing an appetizer is something most cooks have agonized over at some time. As the introduction to a meal, the first course gets the taste buds going and sets the scene for what is to follow. Contrary to popular belief, however, this need not make the task a difficult one.

One of the most important rules is not to overcomplicate things by choosing contrasting flavors or those from vastly different cuisines. In this chapter you will find appetizers from as far afield as Mexico and Thailand, and it would be a brave cook who mixed these cuisines at random. It can be done, of course, but it takes skill and a good bit of foreknowledge of what the end result of the recipe is going to be. It is best then, certainly for the inexperienced cook, to choose an appetizer and entrèe from similar cuisines.

Texture and bulkiness also need to be considered. It would be unwise, for instance, to serve Beef and Bean Soup followed by Chili con Carne. Not only are the flavors too similar, but your guests would be so full they would be falling asleep by the end of the meal! Remember too, not to serve too much of the same ingredient, as well as flavor. If you are having a very meaty main course then serve an appetizer which is mainly vegetable or if you are serving mussels as an appetizer avoid following it with a fish stew – unless, of course, you're hosting a dinner for fish fanatics.

One thing which many cooks forget is that they too are supposed to enjoy the meal. It is very easy to become swamped by the feeling that you have to produce as complicated and impressive a meal as possible. This is most definitely not the best approach. If you have committed yourself to produce a meal of many courses it is vital to organize yourself so that you are not going to spend the entire evening in the kitchen. After all, your guests are there to enjoy your company. Choosing an appetizer that can be made in advance, such as a soup, or one that can be quickly prepared and then put in the oven – Barbecued Ribs are perfect for this purpose – gives the cook time to concentrate on the other parts of the meal. If you would prefer to serve a complicated appetizer then choose a simple entrèe or dessert.

Serving hot and spicy appetizers is one of the best ways to awaken the taste buds, and many of the recipes in this chapter, such as Spicy Shrimp Wraps, Satay Chicken, and Crab Meat Balls, also make ideal fingerfood and snacks. If you are serving a variety of such treats for a drinks party, though, be prepared to make plenty as spicy little nibbles mix wonderfully with drinks and your guests may well be particularly voracious when their tastebuds have been so tantalized.

The recipes in this chapter are among some of the most delicious from around the world, so go ahead and experiment – you'll find the only problem is leaving yourself enough room for the next course!

Chili Rellenos

Organization is the key to preparing these stuffed peppers. Fried inside their golden batter coating, they're puffy and light.

SERVES 8

Full quantity Red Sauce (see recipe for Southwestern Stir-fry page 81)
8 small green bell peppers
4 small green chilies, seeded and finely chopped
1 clove garlic, finely chopped
1 tsp chopped fresh sage
8 oz cream cheese
2 cups grated mild cheese
Salt
Flour for dredging
Oil for deep frying
8 eggs, separated
6 Tbsps all-purpose flour
Pinch of salt
Finely chopped green onions

Blanch the whole peppers in boiling water for about 10-15 minutes, or until just tender. Rinse them in cold water and pat dry. Carefully cut around the stems to make a top, remove and set aside. Scoop out the seeds and cores, leaving the peppers whole. Leave upside down on paper towels to drain.

Mix together the chilies, garlic, sage, cheeses, and salt to taste. Fill the peppers using a teaspoon and replace the tops, pushing them into the filling.

Dredge the peppers with flour and heat the oil in a deep fat fryer to 375°F. Beat the egg yolks and flour in a mixing bowl until the mixture forms a ribbon trail when the beaters are lifted. Beat the whites with a pinch of salt until stiff but not dry. Fold into the egg yolk mixture. Shape 2 tablespoons of batter into an oval and drop into the oil. Immediately slide a metal draining spoon under the batter to hold it in place. Place a filled pepper on the spoon. Cover the tops of the peppers with more batter and then spoon over hot oil to seal. Fry until the batter is brown on all sides, turning the peppers over carefully. Drain on paper towels and keep them warm on a rack in a moderate oven while frying the remaining peppers. Sprinkle with onions and serve with Red Sauce.

Time: Preparation takes about 30 minutes and cooking takes about 3 minutes per pepper.

Hot & Sour Soup

A very warming soup, this is a favorite in winter in Beijing.

SERVES 4-6

2 oz pork tenderloin, very thinly sliced

3 dried Chinese mushrooms, soaked in boiling water for

5 minutes, and chopped

2 oz peeled, uncooked shrimp

5 cups chicken stock

1 oz bamboo shoots, sliced

3 green onions, finely chopped

Salt and freshly ground black pepper

1 Tbsp sugar

½ tsp dark soy sauce

1-2 tsps chili sauce

1½ Tbsps vinegar

Dash sesame seed oil and rice wine or sherry

1 egg, well beaten

2 Tbsps water mixed with 1 Tbsp cornstarch

Place the pork in a large pot with the shrimp and stock. Bring to a boil and then reduce the heat and simmer gently for 4-5 minutes. Add all the remaining ingredients, except for the egg and cornstarch and water mixture. Cook 1-2 minutes over low heat. Remove the pan from the heat and add the egg gradually, stirring gently until it forms threads in the soup. Mix a spoonful of the hot soup with the cornstarch and water mixture and add to the soup, stirring constantly. Bring back to simmering point for 1 minute and serve.

Time: Preparation takes about 25 minutes and cooking takes 7-8 minutes.

Crab Meat Balls

This recipe turns crab meat into a tasty snack.

SERVES 6-8

1 pound fresh or frozen crab meat, finely chopped

4 slices white bread, crusts removed and made into crumbs

1 Tbsp butter or margarine

1 Tbsp all-purpose flour

½ cup milk

½ red or green chili, seeded and finely chopped

1 green onion, finely chopped

1 Tbsp chopped parsley

Salt

Flour

2 eggs, beaten

Dry bread crumbs

Oil for deep frying

Combine the crab meat with the fresh bread crumbs and set aside. Melt the butter in a pan and add the flour off the heat. Stir in the milk and return to moderate heat. Bring to a boil, stirring constantly. Stir the sauce into the crab adding the chili, onion, and parsley. Season to taste, cover and cool completely. Shape the cold crab meat mixture into 1-inch balls using floured hands. Coat with beaten egg using a pastry brush, then coat with the dry bread crumbs. Heat oil in a deep sauté pan, or deep-fat fryer to 350°F. Cook for 3 minutes in batches of 6, turning occasionally, or until golden and crisp. Drain and sprinkle lightly with salt.

Time: Preparation takes 40 minutes and cooking takes about 3 minutes per batch.

Chimichangas

Chimichangas are delicious deep-fried tortilla parcels containing chili, onions, and cheese.

SERVES 6

6 flour tortillas (see page 84)
½ quantity Chili con Carne recipe (see page 71)
6 lettuce leaves, shredded
6 green onions, chopped
3 oz cheddar cheese, shredded
Oil for frying
½ quantity Guacamole recipe (see page 22)
½ cup sour cream
1 tomato, seeded and chopped

Wrap the tortillas in foil and place in a warm oven for 5 minutes to make them pliable. Heat the chili briefly and spoon about 2 tablespoons onto the center of each tortilla. Top with lettuce, onions, and cheese. Fold in the sides to make a parcel, making sure all the filling is enclosed. Heat about 1 inch of oil in a large sauté pan and when hot lower in the chimichangas, folded side down first. Cook 2-4 at a time depending on the size of the pan. Cook for 3 minutes and carefully turn over. Cook a further 3 minutes and remove to paper towels and drain. Repeat with remaining chimichangas. Spoon the guacamole over the top of each and drizzle over the sour cream. Sprinkle over the chopped tomato and serve immediately.

Time: Preparation takes about 30 minutes and cooking takes 15-20 minutes.

Barbecued Ribs

Barbecued meats served with a sweet and spicy sauce are perfect outdoor fare. Here, the meat is prepared in the oven for year-round convenience.

SERVES 6

4½ pounds pork spare ribs
Sauce
1 cup tomato ketchup
2 tsps mustard powder
4 Tbsps Worcestershire sauce
2 Tbsps vinegar
4 Tbsps brown sugar
½ chili, seeded and finely chopped
½ small onion, finely chopped

4 Tbsps water
Salt (if necessary)

Place the ribs in a roasting pan and cover with foil. Cook in a preheated 425°F oven for 15 minutes. Meanwhile, combine all the sauce ingredients in a heavy-based pan and bring to a boil. Reduce heat and simmer for about 15 minutes. Reduce the oven temperature to 350°F and uncover the ribs. Pour the sauce over the ribs and bake a further hour, basting frequently. Remove the ribs from the roasting pan and reserve the sauce. Place the ribs on a cutting board and slice into individual rib pieces between the bones. Skim any fat from the surface of the sauce and serve the sauce separately.

Time: Preparation takes 30 minutes and cooking takes about 1 hour 15 minutes.

Spicy Vegetable Fritters

This delicious dish makes an ideal appetizer or interesting snack. Use any favorite vegetables or those that are in season.

SERVES 4-6

1 cup all-purpose flour

1 cup whole-wheat flour

1½ tsps salt

1 tsp chili powder

1½ tsps ground cumin

1¼ cups water

1½ Tbsps lemon juice

1 small cauliflower, broken into small flowerets

1 eggplant, cut into 1-inch cubes

3 zucchini, cut into 1-inch pieces

2 cups button mushrooms

1 red bell pepper, cut into ¼-inch rounds

1 green bell pepper, cut into ¼-inch rounds

1 large potato, peeled and cut into 1-inch cubes

1⅔ cups canned plum tomatoes, drained

1 red chili, seeded and chopped

1 clove garlic, finely chopped

1 small onion, finely chopped

1½ Tbsps white wine vinegar

1½ Tbsps soft brown sugar

Salt and freshly ground black pepper

1 sliced green chili, to garnish

1 sliced red chili, to garnish

Put the flours, salt, chili powder, and cumin into a large bowl. Make a slight well in the center and gradually add the water and lemon juice to the flour, beating well until a smooth batter is formed. Wash the fresh vegetables and allow them to drain completely on paper towels or a clean cloth. Put the tomatoes, fresh chili, garlic, onions, vinegar, and sugar into a food processor or blender and blend until the sauce is smooth. Pour the sauce mixture into a small pan and heat gently, stirring until it is completely warmed through. Season, transfer to a small serving dish and garnish with slices of red and green chilies.

Heat some oil in a deep fat fryer until it is warm enough to brown a 1-inch cube of bread in just under 1 minute. Make sure the vegetables are completely dry, patting any moisture off them with paper towels if necessary. Using a slotted spoon, drop the vegetables, a few at a time, into the batter and dip them to coat thoroughly. Remove the vegetables from the batter, again using the slotted spoon, and allow some of the batter to drain back into the bowl. Drop the vegetables into the hot oil, and fry quickly until they are golden brown and the batter puffy. Remove the fried vegetables from the oil and drain completely on paper towels, keeping them warm until all the remaining vegetables have been prepared in this manner. Serve immediately with the sauce.

Time: Preparation takes about 20 minutes and cooking takes about ½ hour.

Satay Chicken

This typical Indonesian dish is very spicy and makes an excellent appetizer for four.

SERVES 4

3 Tbsps soy sauce

3 Tbsps sesame oil

3 Tbsps lime juice

1½ tsps ground cumin

1½ tsps turmeric

3 tsps ground coriander

1 pound chicken breast meat, cut into 1-inch cubes

3 Tbsps peanut oil

1 small onion, finely chopped

1½ tsps chili powder

½ cup crunchy peanut butter

1½ tsps brown sugar

Lime wedges and coriander sprigs, to garnish

Put the soy sauce, sesame oil, lime juice, cumin, turmeric, and coriander into a large bowl and mix well. Add the cubed chicken to the soy sauce marinade and stir well to coat the meat evenly. Cover with plastic wrap and allow to stand in a refrigerator for at least 1 hour, but preferably overnight.

Drain the meat, reserving the marinade. Thread the meat onto 4 large or 8 small skewers and set aside. Heat the peanut oil in a small saucepan and add the onion and chili powder. Cook gently until the onion is slightly softened. Stir the reserved marinade into the oil and onion mixture, along with the peanut butter and brown sugar. Heat gently, stirring constantly, until all the ingredients are well blended. If the sauce is too thick, stir in 2-4 tablespoons boiling water.

Arrange the skewers of meat on a broiler pan and cook under a preheated moderate broiler for 10-15 minutes. After the first 5 minutes of cooking, brush the skewered meat with a little of the peanut sauce to baste. During the cooking time turn the meat frequently to cook it on all sides and prevent it browning. Serve the skewered meat garnished with the lime and coriander sprigs, and the remaining sauce in a separate dish.

Time: Preparation takes about 25 minutes and cooking takes about 15 minutes.

Variation: Use a selection of fresh vegetables instead of the chicken to make a vegetarian alternative.

Chili Vegetable Soup

Chilies and lime juice give this soup the startling sharp flavors typical of Tex-Mex cooking.

SERVES 4

1 Tbsp oil

1 onion, chopped

4 oz canned whole green chilies, quartered

4 cups chicken broth

1 large potato, peeled and cut into short strips

Full quantity Taco Sauce recipe (see page 67)

1 Tbsp lime juice

Salt

Tortilla chips and lime slices, to garnish

Heat the oil in a large saucepan and sauté the onion until translucent. Add the green chilies, broth, potato, and taco sauce. Cover the pan and simmer the soup for 20 minutes. Stir in the lime juice and add salt. Serve in individual bowls with tortilla chips. Cut a thin slice of lime to float in each bowl of soup.

Time: Preparation takes about 15 minutes and cooking takes 20 minutes.

Variation: Substitute green bell pepper for half the chilies for a less fiery flavor.

Spicy Shrimp Wraps

Use large, uncooked shrimp for this dish.

SERVES 4

12 raw jumbo shrimp

1 clove garlic, finely chopped

1 stem lemon grass, finely sliced

1 red chili, seeded and chopped

1 tsp grated fresh ginger root

Juice of 1 lime

12 small spring roll wrappers

Oil for deep frying

Peel the shrimp, removing their heads and body shells, but leaving the tail attached. Remove the dark vein and butterfly the shrimp by cutting through the back of them without cutting right through the bodies. Carefully open the shrimp out. Combine the garlic, lemon grass, chili, ginger, and lime juice in a shallow dish and add the shrimp. Turn the shrimp so that they are coated in the marinade, then allow to marinate in the refrigerator for 2 hours, turning occasionally. Just before serving, remove the shrimp from the marinade and wrap each one in a spring roll wrapper, leaving the tail end sticking out. Heat the oil to 350°F in a wok and fry the shrimp wraps in batches for 3-4 minutes or until golden. Drain on paper towels.

Time: Preparation takes 20 minutes, plus 2 hours marinating. Cooking takes about 12 minutes.

Serving idea: Serve with a hot dipping sauce such as chili, or try a hot salsa.

Empanadas

This recipe has been adapted from the Spanish pastries popular in Mexico.

MAKES 6

Triple quantity pastry recipe from Chili Shrimp Quiche (see page 35)

1 egg

Filling

1 onion, chopped

1 clove garlic, finely chopped

1 small green bell pepper, chopped

1 Tbsp oil

8 oz ground beef

1 tsp unsweetened cocoa

1 Tbsp all-purpose flour

½ tsp ground cumin

½ tsp paprika

½ tsp dried oregano, crushed

Salt and freshly ground black pepper

1-2 chilies, seeded and chopped

2 Tbsps tomato paste

3 Tbsps water

2 Tbsps sliced almonds

2 Tbsps raisins

Prepare the pastry according to the recipe for Chili Shrimp Quiche. Cook the onion, garlic, and bell pepper in the oil in a skillet until soft but not colored. Add the meat and fry quickly until well browned. Add the cocoa, flour, spices, oregano, and seasonings. Stir well and cook briefly before adding the chilies, tomato paste, and water. Cook slowly for 10-15 minutes. Add nuts and raisins and allow to cool.

Roll out the pastry on a floured surface and cut out 6 rounds using a 6-inch plate as a guide. Place the cooled filling on one side of the rounds of pastry and dampen the edges with water. Fold over and press to seal the edges. Crimp the edges if desired. Place on cookie sheets and brush with a mixture of beaten egg and salt. Make sure the egg glaze is brushed on evenly. Prick once or twice with a fork and bake in a preheated 425˚F oven for about 15 minutes, or until golden brown.

Time: Preparation takes about 30 minutes and cooking takes about 30 minutes in total.

Mushroom Bhaji

Although mushrooms are not widely used in India, their texture complements spices perfectly.

SERVES 4

3-4 Tbsps oil
1 medium onion, finely chopped
2-3 cloves garlic, finely chopped
½ tsp turmeric
½ tsp chili powder
1 tsp ground coriander
1 tsp ground cumin
¾ tsp salt or to taste
1 Tbsp tomato paste
2 cups button mushrooms

Heat the oil over medium heat and fry the onions until they are lightly browned. Lower heat and add the garlic, turmeric, chili powder, coriander, and cumin. Stir and fry the spices and add about 1 tablespoon water to prevent the spices from sticking to the bottom of the pan. As soon as this water dries up, add a little more. Continue until you have fried the spices for about 5 minutes. Add the salt and tomato paste, mix well and add the mushrooms. Stir until the ingredients are thoroughly mixed. Sprinkle about 2 tablespoons water and cover the pan. Simmer for 10 minutes. The finished dish should have a little amount of sauce, but it should not be runny. If necessary, take the lid off and cook quickly until the sauce is reasonably thick.

Time: Preparation takes 15 minutes and cooking takes 20 minutes.

Nachos

These make excellent cocktail savories. It is best to make them at the last minute as tortilla chips become soggy if topped too soon before serving.

SERVES 8-10

1 package round tortilla chips
1 can refried beans
Full quantity Taco Sauce recipe (see page 67)
1 can Jalapeño bean dip
8-10 cherry tomatoes, sliced
½ cup sour cream or plain yogurt
Sliced black and stuffed green olives
Shredded Cheddar cheese

Taco filling
2 tsps oil
8 oz ground beef
2 tsps chili powder
Pinch of ground coriander
Pinch of cayenne pepper
Salt and freshly ground black pepper

Prepare taco filling as for Tacos recipe. Top half of the tortilla chips with refried beans and half with beef taco filling. Place a spoonful of taco sauce on the bean-topped chips and Jalapeño bean dip in the beef-topped chips. Top the tortilla chips with tomatoes, sour cream or yogurt, olives or cheese in any desired combination, and serve.

Time: Preparation takes about 25 minutes.

Mussels in Chili Sauce

The simple chili sauce in this Thai recipe complements the mussels well.

SERVES 4

2 pounds mussels

1¼ cups water

1 stem lemon grass, chopped

1-inch piece fresh ginger root, peeled and sliced

4 dried kaffir lime leaves

Chili sauce

3 large red chilies, seeded and chopped

1 Tbsp chopped coriander root and stem

2 cloves garlic, finely chopped

2 Tbsps oil

2 Tbsps fish sauce

1 Tbsp sugar

1 Tbsp fresh basil leaves, chopped

2 tsps cornstarch mixed with a little water

Scrub the mussels and remove the beards, discarding any mussels with broken shells or those that do not close when tapped. Bring the water to a boil and add the lemon grass, ginger, and lime leaves. Add the mussels, cover and boil for 5-6 minutes or until the mussels open. Drain, reserving ⅔ cup of the cooking liquid. Discard any mussels that have not opened.

While the mussels are cooking, start to prepare the sauce. Pound the chilies, coriander, and garlic together in a pestle and mortar. Heat the oil in a wok and fry the chili mixture for a few minutes, then stir in the fish sauce, sugar, and basil.

Add the reserved cooking liquid from the mussels and the cornstarch mixture. Cook until slightly thickened. Serve the mussels with the sauce poured over them.

Time: Preparation takes 10 minutes and cooking takes 10-12 minutes.

Watchpoint: Do not overcook the mussels as they will become tough. Remove from the heat as soon as they open.

Seviche

In this traditional Mexican dish the raw fish is "cooked" in a mixture of oil and lime juice. Quick and easy to prepare, seviche makes a highly nutritious and very tasty appetizer.

SERVES 4

1 pound cod fillets
Juice and grated rind of 2 limes
1 small shallot, finely chopped
1 green chili, seeded and finely chopped
1¼ tsps ground coriander
1 small green bell pepper, sliced
1 small red bell pepper, sliced
1¼ Tbsps chopped fresh parsley
1¼ Tbsps chopped fresh coriander
4 green onions, finely chopped
2½ Tbsps olive oil
Freshly ground black pepper
1 small lettuce, to serve

Carefully remove the skin from the cod fillets. Using a sharp knife, cut the fish into very thin strips across the grain. Put the fish strips into a large bowl and pour over the lime juice. Stir in the grated lime rind, shallot, chili, and ground coriander. Mix well. Cover the bowl with plastic wrap and refrigerate for 24 hours, stirring occasionally during this time to ensure that the fish remains well coated in the lime juice.

Mix the sliced peppers, green onions, and fresh herbs together in a large bowl. Put the fish mixture into a colander and drain off the juice. Put the drained fish into the pepper mixture and stir in the oil, mixing well to coat evenly. Add freshly ground pepper to taste. Finely shred the lettuce and arrange on a serving plate. Spread the fish mixture attractively over the lettuce and serve immediately, garnished with slices of lime.

Time: Preparation takes 20 minutes, plus 24 hours standing time.

Variation: Use salmon in place of the cod in this recipe.

Guacamole

Guacamole is the perfect foil for spicy foods.

SERVES 6-8

1 medium onion, finely chopped
1 clove garlic, finely chopped
Grated rind and juice of ½ lime
½ quantity Taco Sauce recipe (see page 67)
3 large avocados
Pinch of salt
1 Tbsp chopped fresh coriander
Coriander sprigs, to garnish

Mix the onion, garlic, rind and juice of lime, and the taco sauce together in a large mixing bowl. Cut the avocados in half lengthwise. Twist the halves gently in opposite directions to separate. Hit the stone with a large, sharp knife and twist the embedded knife to remove the stone. Place the avocado halves cut side down on a chopping board. Lightly score the skin lengthwise and gently pull back to peel. Alternatively, scoop out avocado flesh with a spoon, scraping the skin well. Chop the avocado roughly and immediately place in the bowl with the onion and lime. Use a potato masher to break up the avocado until almost smooth. Do not over-mash. Season with salt and stir in the chopped coriander. Spoon into a serving bowl and garnish with coriander sprigs.

Time: Preparation takes about 25 minutes.
Cooks tip: Guacamole is best made just before it is served as the avocado discolors quickly.

Beef & Bean Soup

The use of refried beans in this recipe has the dual purpose of adding extra flavor and thickening this hearty soup.

SERVES 4

1 large onion, finely chopped
1 red bell pepper, finely chopped
2 stalks celery, chopped
2 Tbsps oil
8oz ground beef
6 tomatoes, peeled, seeded and chopped
15 oz canned refried beans
1 tsp ground cumin
1 tsp chili powder
Pinch of cinnamon and cayenne pepper
1 tsp garlic powder or paste
Salt and freshly ground black pepper
2 cups beef broth

Fry the onion, bell pepper, and celery in the oil in a large saucepan until softened. Add the beef and fry over medium heat until well browned. Add the tomatoes and refried beans with the spices, garlic, and seasoning and mix well. Stir in the broth and bring to a boil. Cover and simmer gently for 30 minutes, stirring occasionally. Pour the soup into a blender or food processor and purée. The soup will be quite thick and not completely smooth. Adjust the seasoning and serve with tortilla chips. Top with sour cream if desired.

Time: Preparation takes about 15 minutes and cooking takes 40 minutes.

Samosas

These crispy vegetable-stuffed triangles can be eaten either hot or cold.

SERVES 6

Dough

2½ cups all-purpose flour

¼ tsp salt

¼ tsp baking powder

½ cup water, to mix

Filling

3 Tbsps oil

1 medium onion, chopped

1 pound potatoes, scrubbed and cut into small dice

2 carrots, grated

¼ cup peas, shelled

¼ cup green beans, chopped

1 tsp chili powder

1 tsp salt

1 tsp garam masala

½ tsp turmeric

1 Tbsp lemon juice

Oil for deep frying

Make the dough by sifting the flour, salt, and baking powder into a bowl and adding the water, a little at a time, to mix to a soft, pliable dough. Cover and leave to stand for 30 minutes.

Heat the 3 tablespoons oil and fry the onion gently, until it is just soft. Stir in the potatoes and carrots and cook for 3-4 minutes. Add the peas and beans to the potato mixture, cook for a further 2 minutes, then stir in the spices and lemon juice. Cover and simmer until the potatoes are tender. Remove from the heat and allow to cool. Divide the dough into 12 equal-sized balls. Roll each piece out on a floured board, to a thin circle about 6 inches in diameter. Cut each circle in half. Dampen the straight edges of each semicircle and bring them together, overlapping slightly to make a cone. Fill each cone as it is made with a little of the filling, then dampen the open edge and seal by pressing together firmly. For extra firmness you may want to dampen and fold this edge over. Heat the oil and fry the samosas, a few at a time, until they are golden brown on both sides. Drain on paper towels.

Time: Preparation takes about 40 minutes and cooking takes about 25 minutes.

Watchpoint: Be careful when using chili powder, not to get it into the eyes. If this happens, rinse the eyes thoroughly with plenty of cold water.

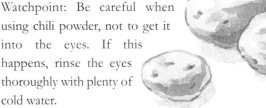

Shrimp Acapulco

Shrimp laced with spices make an exciting appetizer or, if the bread is cut smaller, they can be served with cocktails.

SERVES 4

4 slices bread, crusts removed
6 Tbsps softened butter
6 oz cooked and peeled shrimp
½ tsp chili powder
¼ tsp paprika
¼ tsp cumin
Salt and freshly ground black pepper
Watercress, to garnish

Cut the bread slices in half and spread with 2 tablespoons of the butter. Butter both sides sparingly. Place the bread on a cookie sheet and cook in a preheated 350°F oven for 10-15 minutes until golden brown. Keep warm. Melt the remaining butter in a small pan and add the shrimp, spices, and seasoning and stir well. Heat through for about 3 minutes, remove, and spoon onto the bread slices. Garnish with watercress and serve.

Time: Preparation takes about 15 minutes, cooking takes about 20 minutes.

Watchpoint: Do not heat the shrimp too long or on too high a heat as they toughen easily.

Thai Spring Rolls

Spring rolls are surprisingly simple to make at home.

MAKES ABOUT 12

2 Tbsps oil
1 clove garlic, finely chopped
4 oz chopped pork
2 carrots, cut into thin sticks
2 stalks celery, cut into thin sticks
1 red or green chili, chopped
4 green onions, sliced
1 tsp grated fresh ginger root
1 Tbsp chopped fresh coriander
1 tsp fish sauce
2 oz noodles, cooked
12 spring roll wrappers
Oil for deep frying
Fresh coriander sprigs, to garnish

Heat the oil in a wok or skillet and fry the garlic, pork, carrots, celery, and chili for a few minutes until the pork is cooked. Stir in the green onions, ginger, coriander, fish sauce, and noodles, and cook gently to heat through. Place a spring roll wrapper on a work surface and position a small amount of the filling across one corner. Roll up, folding in the corners to completely enclose the filling. Fill one spring roll at a time and keep the remaining wrappers covered with a damp tea-towel to prevent them from drying out. Just before serving, deep-fry the spring rolls in batches for 3-4 minutes or until crisp and golden. Garnish with coriander sprigs and serve immediately.

Time: Preparation takes 20 minutes and cooking takes 20 minutes.

Chicken Tikka

Chicken Tikka is one of the most popular chicken dishes cooked in the Tandoor, the Indian clay oven. This recipe is adapted to cook the chicken in the conventional oven at a high temperature.

SERVES 4

1 pound boneless, skinned chicken breasts

1 tsp salt

Juice of ½ a lemon

½ tsp tandoori color or a few drops of red food coloring mixed with

1 Tbsp tomato paste

2 cloves garlic, coarsely chopped

½ inch cube fresh ginger root, peeled and coarsely chopped

2 tsps ground coriander

½ tsp ground allspice or garam masala

¼ of a whole nutmeg, finely grated

½ tsp turmeric

⅔ cup thick set plain yogurt

4 Tbsps oil

½ tsp chili powder

Cut the chicken into 1-inch cubes. Sprinkle with ½ tablespoon salt from the specified amount, and the lemon juice; mix thoroughly, cover and set aside for 30 minutes.

Put the rest of the ingredients into a food processor or blender and blend until smooth. Put this marinade into a strainer and hold the strainer over the chicken pieces. Press the marinade through with the back of a metal spoon until only a very coarse mixture is left. Coat the chicken thoroughly with the strained marinade, cover the container and leave to marinate for 6-8 hours or overnight in the refrigerator.

Line a roasting pan with aluminum foil (this will help to maintain the high level of temperature required to cook the chicken quickly without drying it out). Thread the chicken onto skewers, leaving ¼-inch gap between each piece. Place the skewers in the prepared roasting pan and brush with some of the remaining marinade. Cook in the center of a preheated 450°F oven for 6-8 minutes. Take the pan out of the oven, turn the skewers over and brush the pieces of chicken with the remaining marinade. Return the pan to the oven and cook for 6-8 minutes. Shake off any excess liquid from the chicken.

Place the skewers on a serving dish. You make take the tikka off the skewers if you wish, but allow the meat to cool slightly before removing from the skewers.

Time: Preparation takes 30-35 minutes plus time needed to marinate. Cooking takes 15-18 minutes.

Fish & Seafood

Most of us enjoy fish and seafood and, thankfully, the variety and quality now available is beginning to reflect this new found popularity. Much of this growth is due to the promotion of fish, in particular, as a healthfood: it is high in protein, low in fat, and it is thought that oily fish may actually have a part to play in preventing heart disease. Add to this the fact that fish and seafood is versatile, delicious, and quick cooking and you have the perfect food for the nineties.

In the past, many cooks have avoided fish and seafood simply because they were unsure of what to do with it. This was caused by the mistaken belief that it was somehow difficult. A plethora of books and cooks all advising on the ease of preparation and the joys to be had from fresh fish and seafood have gone someway to redressing this, but probably of more influence is the wider availability of ready-cleaned and prepared produce.

Fish and seafood may be more readily available but it is most certainly not always of the high standard required to produce a really first class dish. Freshness is vital. If you can possibly buy your fish or shellfish fresh rather than frozen then do so, but make sure it really is fresh. Fish should be bright and shiny with firm flesh; the eyes should be rounded and bright, not dull and sunken; and the gills should be a bright red. As a fish ages the gills go a grayish color so watch out for this as a sign of a fish that is definitely past its best. The same guidelines apply to shellfish as fish; it is almost always best to buy it fresh. Frozen shellfish is invariably coated with ice which melts away to leave a product that often bears little resemblance to its frozen appearance or weight.

Fish and seafood combine well with hot and spicy ingredients, although a little care needs to be taken if its flavor is not to be overpowered by other ingredients. For this reason many of these recipes feature fish and seafood which have a robust flavor or those with a flavor that is enhanced by a hot and spicy accompaniment. Spiced Sardines is the perfect example of a recipe in which the flavor of the fish is enhanced by a particularly strong blend of spices. Shrimp also takes well to this type of treatment, whereas bream requires a more gentle approach and is accompanied with a subtle sweet and sour sauce in our recipe.

From Chili Shrimp Quiche to Shrimp with Cashew Nuts, and Chilled Fish Curry, the various approaches taken to combining fish and seafood with hot and spicy ingredients in this chapter illustrate just how easy it is to be creative with one of the most delicious bounties nature has to offer.

Plaice with Spicy Tomato Sauce

This spicy Tex-Mex dish is perfect for entertaining. With Mexico and Texas both bordering the Gulf of Mexico it's logical that the region's cooking should include fish in its repertoire.

SERVES 4

3 oz cream cheese

1 tsp dried oregano

Pinch of cayenne pepper

4 whole fillets plaice

Lime slices and dill, to garnish

Tomato sauce

1 Tbsp oil

1 small onion, chopped

1 stalk celery, chopped

1 chili, seeded and chopped

¼ tsp each ground cumin, coriander and ginger

½ red and ½ green bell pepper, chopped

14 oz canned tomatoes

1 Tbsp tomato paste

Salt, freshly ground black pepper, and a pinch of sugar

To prepare the sauce, heat the oil in a heavy-based pan and cook the onion, celery, chili, and spices for about 5 minutes over very low heat. Add the bell peppers and the remaining sauce ingredients and bring to a boil. Reduce heat and simmer 15-20 minutes, stirring occasionally. Set aside while preparing the fish.

Mix the cream cheese, oregano, and cayenne pepper together and set aside. Skin the fillets using a filletting knife. Start at the tail end and hold the knife at a slight angle to the skin. Push the knife along using a sawing motion, with the blade against the skin. Dip fingers in salt to make it easier to hold onto the fish skin. Gradually separate the fish from the skin. Spread the cheese filling on all 4 fillets and roll each up. Secure with wooden picks.

Place the fillets in a lightly greased baking pan, cover and cook in a preheated 350°F oven for 10 minutes. Pour over the tomato sauce and cook a further 10-15 minutes. Fish is cooked when it feels firm and looks opaque. Garnish with lime slices and dill.

Time: Preparation takes about 30 minutes and cooking takes 20-25 minutes.

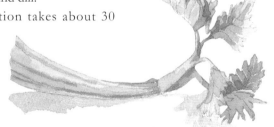

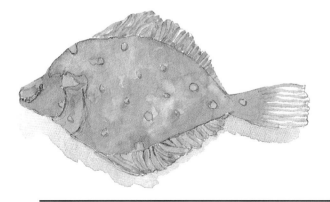

Spiced Sardines

If fresh sardines are not available use any other small, whole
fish. This recipe couldn't be easier or
more delicious.

SERVES 4

8 fresh sardines (about 1½ pounds)

1 tsp salt or to taste

3-4 cloves garlic, coarsely chopped

Juice of half a lemon

½ tsp turmeric

½-1 tsp chili powder

3 heaped Tbsps all-purpose flour

⅓ cup oil

Scale and clean the fish, if necessary. Wash gently in cold water
and dry on paper towels. Add the salt to the garlic and crush
to a smooth pulp. Mix all the ingredients together, except the fish,
flour, and oil, in a small bowl. Put the fish in a wide shallow dish
and pour the marinade over. Spread it gently on both sides of the
fish, cover and refrigerate for 2-4 hours. Heat the oil over medium
heat. Dip each fish in the flour and coat it thoroughly. Fry until
golden brown on both sides (2-3 minutes each side). Drain on
paper towels.

Time: Preparation takes 20 minutes plus 2-
4 hours to marinate, cooking takes
6-8 minutes.
Serving idea: Serve with crusty bread and a
tomato salad.

Chilled Fish Curry

This sophisticated, mild curry will serve four as a refreshing
summer lunch, or eight as an elegant appetizer.

SERVES 4-8

8 oz fresh salmon fillet

12 oz whitefish fillet

Chicken broth

Salt and freshly ground black pepper

½ cup mayonnaise

1 cup plain yogurt

2 tsps curry powder

Juice and grated rind of ½ lemon

¾ cup peeled shrimp

Garnish

Kiwi fruit, peeled and sliced

Sprigs of fresh mint

Flaked coconut

Put the salmon and whitefish fillets into a shallow pan and add
just enough chicken broth to cover. Season to taste and
simmer gently until the fish is just tender – about 4-6 minutes.
Remove the fish carefully from the cooking liquor and leave to
cool slightly. In a medium-sized bowl, mix together the
mayonnaise and yogurt. Blend in the curry powder, lemon juice,
and rind. Flake the cooked fish, removing any bones and skin. Mix
the flaked fish into the curry sauce, together with the shrimp.
Arrange the fish curry on serving plates and garnish with slices of
kiwi fruit, sprigs of fresh mint, and coconut flakes.
Time: Preparation takes about 20 minutes and cooking takes
about 6 minutes.

Seafood Pan Roast

In this recipe, oysters and fresh crab are turned into a dish that is based on the French gratin.

SERVES 4

24 small oysters, on the half shell

1 cup fish broth

1 cup heavy cream

1 large or 2 small cooked crabs

4 slices bread, crusts trimmed, made into crumbs

1/3 cup butter or margarine

6 Tbsps all-purpose flour

1 bunch green onions, chopped

2 oz parsley, chopped

2 Tbsps Worcestershire sauce

1/2 tsp Tabasco sauce

Remove the oysters from their shells, place in a saucepan and strain over any oyster liquid. Add the fish broth and cook gently until the oysters curl around the edges. Remove the oysters, keep them warm and strain the liquid into a clean pan. Add the cream, bring to a boil and boil rapidly for about 5 minutes. Remove the crab's claws and legs. Turn the crab over and push out the body, remove the stomach sac and lungs and discard. Cut the body in four sections and pick out the meat with a skewer. Crack claws and legs to extract the meat. Scrape out the brown meat from inside the shell and combine it with the bread crumbs and white meat from the body and claws.

Melt the butter in a medium saucepan and stir in the flour. Cook gently for 5 minutes. Add the onions and parsley and cook 5 minutes. Pour over the cream mixture, stirring constantly, then bring to a boil. Add the Worcestershire sauce and Tabasco sauce. Cook about 15-20 minutes over low heat, stirring occasionally. Fold in the crab meat mixture and heat for 1-2 minutes. Place the oysters in the bottom of a buttered casserole or in individual dishes and spoon the crab meat mixture on top. Broil to brown, if desired, and serve immediately.

Time: Preparation takes about 40 minutes and cooking takes about 30 minutes.

Shrimp Chili Masala

This is a delicate but richly flavored dish.

SERVES 4

⅓ cup unsalted butter

6 green cardamoms, split open on the top

1-inch cube fresh ginger root, peeled and finely grated

3-4 cloves garlic, finely chopped

1 Tbsp ground coriander

½ tsp turmeric

1 pound raw shrimp

⅔ cup plain yogurt

⅓ cup water

1 tsp sugar

1 tsp salt or to taste

¼ cup ground almonds

4-5 whole green chilies

1 small onion, finely chopped

2 green chilies, seeded and finely chopped

½ tsp garam masala

1 Tbsp chopped fresh coriander

Melt ⅔ of the butter from the specified amount over gentle heat and add the whole cardamoms; fry for 30 seconds and add the ginger and garlic. Stir and cook for 1 minute, then add the ground coriander and turmeric. Stir and fry for 30 seconds. Add the shrimp, turn the heat up to medium and cook for 5-6 minutes, stirring frequently.

Beat the yogurt until smooth, gradually add the water and beat until well blended. Add this mixture to the shrimp, stir in the sugar and the salt, cover the pan and simmer for 5-6 minutes. Add the ground almonds and the whole green chili peppers and cook, uncovered, for 5 minutes.

Meanwhile, fry the onions in the remaining butter until they are just soft, but not brown. Add the finely chopped chilies and the garam masala; stir and fry for a further 1-2 minutes. Stir this mixture into the shrimp along with any butter left in the pan. Remove the pan from the heat. Place in a serving dish and garnish with the coriander or more sliced chilies.

Time: Preparation takes 15 minutes, cooking takes 20-25 minutes.

Gulf Coast Tacos

A tasty variation on beef tacos, this recipe features a delicious seafood filling.

SERVES 6

6 Tortillas (see page 84)
Oil for frying
Green chili salsa
1 Tbsp oil
3 Tomatillos, husks removed
1 clove garlic
1 oz coriander leaves
2 green chilies
Juice of 1 lime
½ cup sour cream
Pinch of salt and sugar
Filling ingredients
8 oz large raw shrimp, peeled
8 oz raw scallops, quartered if large
1 tsp coriander seed, crushed
1 shallot, finely chopped
Salt and freshly ground black pepper
6 Tbsps white wine
1 small jicama root, peeled and cut into thin matchstick strips
Coriander sprigs and lime wedges

Prepare the tortillas according to the recipe. Heat the oil for the salsa in a small skillet and slice the tomatillos. Sauté them for about 3 minutes to soften. Place in a food processor along with the garlic, coriander, chilies, and lime juice. Purée until smooth.

Fold in the sour cream, adjust seasoning and chill. Heat oil in a deep sauté pan to a depth of at least 2 inches. When hot, add a tortilla and press down under the oil with a metal spoon. When the tortilla starts to puff up, take it out and immediately fold in half to form a shell. Hold in shape until it cools slightly and sets. Repeat with the remaining tortillas. Keep them warm in an oven, standing on their open ends to prevent them from closing.

Place the shrimp, scallops, coriander seeds, shallot, and salt and pepper in a sauté pan with enough wine and water to barely cover. Cook for about 8 minutes, stirring occasionally. The shrimp should turn pink and the scallops will look opaque when cooked. Fill the taco shells with the jicama. Remove the seafood from the liquid with a draining spoon and arrange on top of the jicama. Top with the salsa and garnish with coriander sprigs. Serve with lime wedges.

Time: Preparation takes about 1 hour.

Shrimp Veracruz

This colorful and spicy seafood dish is named for the port of Veracruz on the Gulf of Mexico.

SERVES 6

1 Tbsp oil

1 onion, chopped

1 large green bell pepper, cut into 1½-inch strips

2-3 green chilies, seeded and chopped

Double quantity Taco Sauce recipe (see page 67)

2 tomatoes, peeled and roughly chopped

12 pimiento-stuffed olives, halved

2 tsps capers

¼ tsp ground cumin

Salt

1 pound shrimp, uncooked

Juice of 1 lime

Heat the oil in a large skillet and add the onion and bell pepper. Cook until soft but not colored. Add chilies, taco sauce, tomatoes, olives, capers, cumin, and salt. Bring to a boil and then lower the heat to simmer for 5 minutes. Add the shrimp to the sauce and cook for 4-5 minutes, or until they curl up and turn pink and opaque. Add the lime juice to taste and serve.

Time: Preparation takes 25 minutes and cooking takes about 15 minutes.

Preparation: The sauce can be prepared in advance and reheated while the shrimp are cooking.

Bream in Sweet & Sour Sauce

Steamed fillet of sea bream and a spicy sweet and sour sauce are combined in this recipe.

SERVES 4

1 sea bream, 2 pounds, cleaned and filleted

½ red bell pepper and ½ green bell pepper, seeded

¼ cucumber

1 tsp each finely chopped fresh ginger root and garlic

2 green onions, finely chopped

1 Tbsp oil

1 red or green chili, seeded

3 Tbsps pineapple juice

2 Tbsps crushed tomatoes

½ cup fish broth

1 tsp cornstarch, combined with a little water

1 Tbsp vinegar

Salt and freshly ground black pepper

1 Tbsp chopped fresh chives

Cut the bell peppers and the cucumber into fine julienne. Heat the oil in a wok and sauté the vegetables, ginger, garlic, green onions, and chili for 1 minute. Add the pineapple juice, crushed tomato, and fish broth. Simmer over a low heat for 2 minutes. Thicken the sauce with the cornstarch paste, stirring continuously. Discard the chili, add the vinegar, and season with salt and pepper to taste. Steam the bream over water for 5-6 minutes or until just cooked. Serve the fish accompanied with the sweet and sour sauce and sprinkled with the chopped chives.

Time: Preparation takes about 30 minutes and cooking takes about 15 minutes.

Blackened Fish

The fish in this recipe, usually redfish or pompano, should be cooked until it has a very brown crust.

SERVES 4

1 cup unsalted butter

4 fish fillets or steaks, eg. redfish or pompano, about 8 oz each

1 Tbsp paprika

1 tsp garlic powder

1 tsp cayenne pepper

½ tsp ground white pepper

1 tsp finely ground black pepper

2 tsps salt

1 tsp dried thyme

Melt the butter and pour about half into each of four custard cups and set aside. Brush each fish fillet liberally with the remaining butter on both sides. Mix together the spices, seasonings, and thyme and sprinkle generously on each side of the fillets, patting it on by hand.

Heat a skillet and add about 1 tablespoon butter per fish fillet. When the butter is hot, add the fish, skin side down first. Turn the fish over when the underside is very brown and repeat with the remaining side. Add more butter as necessary during cooking. When the top side of the fish is very dark brown, repeat with the remaining fish fillets, keeping them warm while cooking the rest. Serve the fish immediately with the cups of butter for dipping.
Time: Preparation takes about 20 minutes and cooking takes 5 minutes per fillet.

Spiced Salmon Steaks

This easy-to-prepare salmon dish is very out of the ordinary.

SERVES 4

½ cup soft light brown sugar

1 Tbsp ground allspice

1 Tbsp mustard powder

1 Tbsp grated fresh ginger root

4 salmon steaks, 1-inch thick

1 cucumber

1 bunch green onions

2 Tbsps butter

1 Tbsp lemon juice

2 tsps chopped fresh dill weed

1 Tbsp chopped fresh parsley

Salt and freshly ground black pepper

Mix the sugar and spices together and rub the mixture into the surface of both sides of the salmon steaks. Allow the salmon steaks to stand for at least 1 hour in the refrigerator.

Peel the cucumber and cut into quarters lengthways. Remove the seeds and cut each quarter into 1-inch pieces. Trim the roots from the green onions and cut down some, but not all, of the green part. Put the cucumber and green onions into a saucepan, along with the butter, lemon juice, dill, parsley, and seasoning. Cook over a moderate heat for about 10 minutes, or until the cucumber is tender. Put the salmon steaks under a preheated moderate broiler and cook for about 5-6 minutes on each side. Serve with the cucumber and green onion accompaniment.
Time: Preparation takes about 15 minutes, plus standing time of 1 hour, and cooking takes 12-15 minutes.

Chili Shrimp Quiche

Chilies, green onions, and garlic give this shrimp quiche bite and flavor.

SERVES 6

Pastry
1 cup all-purpose flour
2 Tbsps butter or margarine
2 Tbsps vegetable shortening
2-4 Tbsps cold water

Filling
½ cup milk
½ cup light cream
½ clove garlic, finely chopped
Salt
1 cup Cheddar cheese, shredded
3 green onions, chopped
2 green chilies, seeded and chopped
8 oz cooked and peeled shrimp
Cooked, unpeeled shrimp and parsley sprigs to garnish

Sift the flour with a pinch of salt into a mixing bowl, or place in a food processor and mix once or twice. Cut in the butter and shortening until the mixture resembles fine bread crumbs, or work in the food processor, being careful not to over-mix. Mix in the liquid gradually, adding enough to bring the dough together in a ball. In a food processor, add the liquid through the funnel while the machine is running. Wrap the dough well and chill for 20-30 minutes.

Roll out the dough on a well-floured surface with a floured rolling pin. Carefully press the dough onto the bottom of a 10-inch pie pan and up the sides of the pan, taking care not to stretch it. Roll the rolling pin over the top of the pan to remove excess dough, or cut off with a sharp knife. Mix the eggs, milk, cream, and garlic together. Add salt. Sprinkle the cheese, onions, chilies, and shrimp onto the base of the dough and pour over the egg mixture. Bake in a preheated 400°F oven for 30-40 minutes until firm and golden brown. Peel the tail shells off the shrimp and remove the legs and roe if present. Use shrimp to garnish the quiche along with the sprigs of parsley.

Time: Preparation takes 40 minutes and cooking takes 30-40 minutes.

Sichuan Fish

The piquant spiciness of Sichuan pepper is quite different from that of black or white pepper. Beware, though, too much can numb the mouth temporarily!

SERVES 6

1 pound whitefish fillets

Salt and freshly ground black pepper

1 egg

5 Tbsps all-purpose flour

6 Tbsps white wine

Oil for frying

2 oz cooked ham, cut in small dice

1-inch piece fresh ginger root, peeled and finely diced

1 red or green chili, seeded and finely diced

6 water chestnuts, finely diced

4 green onions, finely chopped

3 Tbsps light soy sauce

1 tsp cider vinegar or rice wine vinegar

1/2 tsp ground Sichuan pepper (optional)

1 cup light stock

1 Tbsp cornstarch dissolved with 2 Tbsps water

2 tsps sugar

Cut the fish fillets into 2-inch pieces and season with salt and pepper. Beat the egg well and add flour and wine to make a batter. Dredge the fish lightly with flour and then dip into the batter. Mix the fish well. Heat a wok and, when hot, add enough oil to deep fry the fish. When the oil is hot, fry a few pieces of fish at a time, until golden brown. Drain and continue until all the fish is cooked.

Remove all but 1 tablespoon of oil from the wok and add the ham, ginger, diced chili, water chestnuts, and green onions. Cook for about 1 minute and add the soy sauce and vinegar. If using Sichuan pepper, add at this point. Stir well and cook for 1 minute. Remove the vegetables from the pan and set them aside. Add the broth to the wok and bring to a boil. When boiling, add 1 spoonful of the hot stock to the cornstarch mixture. Add the mixture back to the stock and reboil, stirring constantly until thickened. Stir in the sugar and return the fish and vegetables to the sauce. Heat through for 30 seconds and serve at once.

Time: Preparation takes about 30 minutes and cooking takes about 10 minutes.

Buying Guide: Sichuan peppercorns are available in Chinese supermarkets or delicatessens. If unavailable, substitute extra chilies.

Crawfish Pie

If you cannot buy crawfish for this popular Southern dish, it is quite acceptable to use shrimp.

SERVES 4

Pastry

2 cups all-purpose flour, sifted

Pinch of salt

½-¼ cup butter or margarine

Cold water

½ quantity spice mixture for Shellfish Boil (see page 44)

1 pound peeled, raw crawfish or shrimp

Filling

3 Tbsps oil

3 Tbsps flour

½ green bell pepper, finely diced

2 green onions, finely chopped

1 stalk celery, finely chopped

1 cup heavy cream

Salt and freshly ground black pepper

Sift the flour for the pastry into a bowl with a pinch of salt and cut in the butter or margarine until the mixture resembles fine bread crumbs. Add enough cold water to bring the mixture together. Knead into a ball, wrap well and chill for about 30 minutes before use.

Combine the spice mixture in a saucepan with about 2½ cups water. Bring to a boil and add the crawfish or shrimp. Cook for about 5 minutes, stirring occasionally, until the shellfish curl up. Remove from the liquid and leave to drain. Heat the oil for the filling in a small pan and add the flour. Cook slowly, stirring constantly until the flour turns a rich dark brown. Add the remaining filling ingredients, stirring constantly while adding the cream. Bring to a boil, reduce the heat and cook for 5 minutes. Add the crawfish or shrimp.

Divide the dough into 4 and roll out each portion on a lightly-floured surface to about ¼-inch thick. Line individual pie pans with the dough, pushing it carefully onto the base and up the sides, taking care not to stretch it. Trim off excess dough and reserve. Place a sheet of baking parchment or foil on the dough and pour on baking beans to come halfway up the sides. Bake the dough for 10 minutes in a preheated 400°F oven. Remove the paper and beans and bake for an additional 5 minutes to cook the base. Spoon in the filling and roll out the trimmings to make a lattice pattern on top. Bake for 10 minutes to brown the lattice and heat the filling.

Time: Preparation takes about 30 minutes and cooking takes about 35 minutes in total.

Trout with Chorizo

For fish with a spicy difference, try this as a dinner party dish to impress and please your fish-loving friends.

SERVES 4

1 boned trout (about 2 pound boned weight)
8 oz chorizo or other spicy sausage
Water
1 small green bell pepper, finely chopped
2 small onions, finely chopped
1 slice bread, made into crumbs
4 Tbsps dry white wine
Lemon juice
½ cup plain yogurt
1 tsp garlic powder
2 tsps chopped coriander
Salt and freshly ground black pepper

Place the chorizo in a pan and cover with water. Bring to a boil and then cook for 10 minutes to soften and remove excess fat. Skin sausage and chop it finely. Combine with the green pepper, onion, bread crumbs, and wine. Sprinkle the fish cavity with the lemon juice. Stuff the fish with the sausage mixture and place on lightly-oiled foil. Seal the ends to form a parcel and bake in a preheated 350°F oven for about 20-30 minutes, or until the fish feels firm and the flesh looks opaque. Combine the yogurt, garlic powder, coriander, and seasonings to taste. Remove the fish from the foil and transfer to a serving plate. Spoon some of the sauce over the fish and serve the rest separately.

Time: Preparation takes about 25 minutes and cooking takes about 30 minutes.

Variation: Other whole fish such as sea bass or gray mullet may be used with the stuffing, however, the stuffing is too spicy to use with salmon.

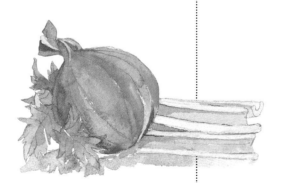

Stir-fried Seafood

Stir-frying is the perfect choice for seafood.

SERVES 4-6

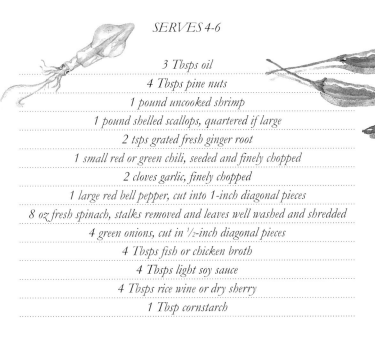

3 Tbsps oil

4 Tbsps pine nuts

1 pound uncooked shrimp

1 pound shelled scallops, quartered if large

2 tsps grated fresh ginger root

1 small red or green chili, seeded and finely chopped

2 cloves garlic, finely chopped

1 large red bell pepper, cut into 1-inch diagonal pieces

8 oz fresh spinach, stalks removed and leaves well washed and shredded

4 green onions, cut in ½-inch diagonal pieces

4 Tbsps fish or chicken broth

4 Tbsps light soy sauce

4 Tbsps rice wine or dry sherry

1 Tbsp cornstarch

Heat oil in a wok and add the pine nuts. Cook over low heat, stirring continuously, until lightly browned. Remove and drain on paper towels. Add the shrimp and scallops to the wok, and stir over moderate heat until shellfish is beginning to look opaque and the shrimp pink. Add the ginger, chili, garlic, and red pepper and cook a few minutes over moderately high heat. Add the spinach and onion, and stir-fry briefly. Mix the remaining ingredients together and add to the wok. Turn up the heat to bring the liquid quickly to a boil, stirring ingredients constantly. Once the liquid thickens and clears, stir in the pine nuts and serve immediately.

Time: Preparation takes about 35 minutes and cooking takes 8-10 minutes.

Shrimp & Scallop Stir-fry

This recipe is from Thailand, where seafood plays a prominent part in the diet.

SERVES 4

1 tsp black peppercorns

1 shallot, chopped

2 small red chilies, sliced

3 cloves garlic, finely chopped

2 Tbsps oil

8 oz peeled raw shrimp

12 oz prepared mixed seafood, e.g. clams, squid, scallops etc.

1 Tbsp fish sauce

1 Tbsp lime juice

4 green onions, sliced

Place the black peppercorns in a pestle and mortar and crush well. Add the shallot, chilies, and garlic and continue to pound until well combined. Heat the oil in a wok, add the chili mixture and stir-fry for 1 minute. Add the shrimp and the other prepared seafood and stir-fry for 3-4 minutes, or until the mixed seafood looks opaque and the shrimp turn pink. Sprinkle with fish sauce and lime juice. Serve scattered with green onion slices.

Time: Preparation takes 10 minutes and cooking takes 5-6 minutes.

Cook's Tip: Prepared mixed seafood can be bought in many large supermarkets.

Creole Court Bouillon

This classic soup-stew is based on fresh fish stock.

SERVES 4

2 whole whitefish, filleted and skinned, skin and bones reserved

1 bay leaf, 1 sprig thyme and 2 parsley stalks

2 slices onion

1 lemon slice

6 black peppercorns

1½ cups water

6 Tbsps oil

6 Tbsps all-purpose flour

1 large green bell pepper, finely chopped

1 onion, finely chopped

1 stalk celery, finely chopped

2 pounds canned tomatoes

2 Tbsps tomato paste

1 tsp cayenne pepper

Pinch of salt and allspice

6 Tbsps white wine

2 Tbsps chopped fresh parsley

Place the skin and bones of the fish in a large pan with the herbs, onion and lemon slices, peppercorns, and water. Bring to a boil, lower the heat and simmer for 20 minutes. Strain and set aside.

Heat the oil in a large saucepan and add the flour. Cook slowly, stirring constantly, until golden brown. Add the bell pepper, onion, and celery. Cook until the flour is a rich dark brown and the vegetables have softened. Strain on the broth, stirring constantly. Add the canned tomatoes, tomato paste, cayenne pepper, salt, and allspice. Bring to a boil and simmer until thick. Add the wine. Cut the fish fillets into 2-inch pieces and add to the tomato mixture. Cook slowly for about 20 minutes, or until the fish is tender. Gently stir in the parsley, taking care that the fish does not break up.

Time: Preparation takes about 30 minutes and cooking takes about 35 minutes.

Caribbean Shrimp & Sweet Potatoes

This recipe makes delicious use of shrimp and sweet potatoes.

SERVES 6

1 pound sweet potatoes, peeled and diced
1 large onion, chopped
1 clove garlic, finely chopped
1-inch piece of fresh ginger root, peeled and grated
1 red or green chili, seeded and chopped
¼ tsp each ground cumin, coriander, and allspice
2 Tbsps coconut cream, OR ½ oz creamed coconut, dissolved in
2 Tbsps boiling water
2 cups water
¾ cup peeled shrimp
4 oz Belgian endive, shredded
8 oz Chinese cabbage, shredded
1 Tbsp dark brown sugar
2 Tbsps lime juice
Salt
Shredded coconut, to sprinkle

In a large saucepan, mix together the sweet potatoes, onions, garlic, ginger, chili, spices, coconut cream, and water. Bring to a boil and simmer until the potato is almost tender. Add the shrimp, Belgian endive, and Chinese cabbage. Simmer for 2-3 minutes, until the ingredients are warmed through, but the leaves are still crisp. Add the sugar and lime juice and season to taste. Serve sprinkled with the shredded coconut.
Time: Preparation takes about 20 minutes and cooking takes 20-25 minutes.

Swordfish with Grapefruit Salsa

Swordfish spiked with the tart flavors of citrus fruits and tequila makes a refreshing delicacy.

SERVES 4

4-6 ruby or pink grapefruit (depending on size)
1 lime
½ green chili, seeded and finely diced
1 green onion, finely chopped
2 Tbsps chopped fresh coriander
1 Tbsp sugar
3 Tbsps tequila
Juice of 1 lime
2 Tbsps oil
Black pepper, to taste
4-8 swordfish steaks (depending on size)
Coriander sprigs for garnish

Remove the zest from the grapefruit and lime with a zester and set it aside. Remove all the pith from the grapefruit and segment them. Squeeze the lime for juice. Mix the grapefruit and citrus zests with the chili, onion, coriander, sugar, tequila, and lime juice and set aside. Mix the remaining lime juice oil, and pepper together and brush both sides of the fish. Place under preheated broiler and cook for about 4 minutes each side, or until the flesh is firm and looks opaque. To serve, place a coriander sprig on each fish steak and serve with the grapefruit salsa.
Time: Preparation takes about 35 minutes and cooking takes 5 minutes.

Shrimp with Cashew Nuts

Cashew nuts give added texture to this chili-flavored dish.

½ tsp chopped fresh ginger root

1 tsp chopped garlic

1½ Tbsps cornstarch

¼ tsp sugar

1 pound uncooked shrimp, peeled

4 Tbsps oil

1 small onion, diced

1 large or 2 small zucchini, cut into ½-inch cubes

1 small red bell pepper, cut into ½-inch cubes

½ cup cashew nuts

Sauce

¾ cup chicken broth

1 Tbsp cornstarch

2 tsps chili sauce

2 tsps sesame oil

1 Tbsp dry sherry or rice wine

Mix together the ginger, garlic, 1½ tablespoons cornstarch, salt, pepper, and sugar. Add the shrimp and leave to stand for 20 minutes. Heat the oil in a wok and cook the shrimp, stirring over high heat for about 20 seconds. Transfer to a plate. Add the onion to the wok and cook for about 1 minute. Add the zucchini and red bell pepper and cook about 30 seconds. Mix the sauce ingredients together and add to the wok. Cook, stirring constantly, until the sauce is slightly thickened. Add the shrimp and cashew nuts and heat 3-4 minutes until shrimp turns pink.
Time: Preparation takes 20 minutes, cooking takes 5 minutes.

Seafood Gumbo Filé

A delicious, hearty dish.

SERVES 6

1 pound cooked, unpeeled shrimp

½ quantity spice mixture for Shellfish Boil (see page 44)

4 Tbsps butter or margarine

1 onion, sliced

1 green bell pepper, sliced

2 cloves garlic, finely chopped

3 Tbsps all-purpose flour

½ tsp thyme

1 bay leaf

2 Tbsps chopped fresh parsley

Dash of Worcestershire sauce

12 oysters, shelled

8 oz tomatoes, peeled and chopped

2 Tbsps filé powder

Peel the shrimp and reserve the shells. Mix the shells with the spice mixture and 5 cups water and bring to a boil in a large stock pot. Reduce the heat and simmer for 20 minutes. Melt the butter and, when foaming, add the onion, bell pepper, garlic, and flour. Cook slowly, stirring constantly until the flour is pale golden brown. Gradually strain on the stock, discarding the shells and spice mixture. Add the thyme and bay leaf and stir well. Bring to a boil and simmer until thick. Add the parsley, Worcestershire sauce, oysters, peeled shrimp and tomatoes. Heat through gently for 5-6 minutes. Stir in the filé powder and leave to stand to thicken.
Time: Preparation takes 30 minutes, cooking takes 25 minutes.

Coconut Fried Fish
– with Chilies –

A real treat for lovers of spicy food.

SERVES 4

Oil for frying

1 pound sole or plaice fillets, skinned, boned and cut into 1-inch strips

Seasoned all-purpose flour

1 egg, beaten

¾ cup shredded coconut

1 Tbsp oil

1 tsp grated fresh ginger root

¼ tsp chili powder

1 red chili, seeded and finely chopped

1 tsp ground coriander

½ tsp ground nutmeg

1 clove garlic, finely chopped

2 Tbsps tomato paste

2 Tbsps tomato chutney

2 Tbsps dark soy sauce

2 Tbsps lemon juice

2 Tbsps water

1 tsp brown sugar

Salt and freshly ground black pepper

In a skillet, heat about 2 inches of oil to 375°F. Toss the fish strips in the seasoned flour and then dip them into the beaten egg. Roll them in the shredded coconut and shake off the excess. Fry the fish, a few pieces at a time, in the hot oil until just crisp and drain on paper towels. Keep warm.

Heat the 1 tablespoon of oil in a wok or skillet and fry the ginger, red chili, spices, and garlic for about 2 minutes. Add the remaining ingredients and simmer for about 3 minutes. Serve the fish, with the sauce handed round separately.

Time: Preparation takes about 30 minutes and cooking takes about 30 minutes.

Serving Idea: Serve with plain boiled rice, a cucumber relish and plenty of salad.

Shrimp, Scallop, & Bacon — Kebabs —

These kebabs are particularly delicious.

SERVES 4

12 large, raw scallops

12 strips Canadian bacon

12 raw jumbo shrimp, peeled and de-veined

Juice of 1 lemon

2 Tbsps oil

Coarsely ground black pepper

Red chili yogurt sauce

3 slices bread, crusts removed, soaked in water

2 cloves garlic, finely chopped

1 red chili, seeded and chopped

1 red bell pepper, grilled and peeled

3 Tbsps olive oil

½ cup plain yogurt

Wrap each scallop in a strip of bacon and thread onto skewers, alternating with the shrimp. Mix the lemon juice, oil, and pepper and brush over the shellfish as they cook. Turn frequently and cook for about 10 minutes until the bacon is lightly crisped and the scallops are just firm.

Squeeze the bread to remove the water and place the bread in a blender. Add the finely chopped garlic, chopped red chili, and skinned red pepper, and blend well. With the machine running, pour in the oil through the funnel in a thin, steady stream and blend until the mixture is a smooth, shiny paste. Combine with the yogurt and mix well. Serve with the kebabs.

Time: Preparation takes 25 minutes and cooking takes 10-15 minutes.

Shellfish Boil

Simple and delicious, this recipe is a great way to satisfy a crowd.

SERVES 4-6

3 quarts water

1 lemon, quartered

1 onion, cut in half but not peeled

1 stalk celery, cut into 3 pieces

2 cloves garlic, left whole

Pinch of salt

4 bay leaves

1 Tbsp dill weed, fresh or dry

4 dried red chilies, crumbled

1 Tbsp each whole cloves, whole allspice, coriander seed and mustard seed (spice mix)

2 tsps celery seed

1 pound raw, unpeeled shrimp

2 pound mussels, well scrubbed

Place the water, lemon, onion, celery, garlic, salt, herbs, and spices together in a large pot and cover. Bring to a boil, reduce the heat and cook slowly for 20 minutes. Add the shrimp in two batches and cook until pink and curled. Remove with a draining spoon. Add the mussels to the pot and cook, stirring frequently, for about 5 minutes or until shells have opened. Discard any that do not open. Spoon shrimp and mussels into serving bowls and serve immediately.

Time: Preparation takes about 30 minutes and cooking takes 25 minutes.

Tandoori Fish

A firm-fleshed whitefish is ideal for this dish. The fish should be handled carefully as most whitefish tends to flake during cooking.

SERVES 4

1 pound fillets or steaks of any whitefish

2 cloves garlic, coarsely chopped

¼-inch cube of fresh ginger root, peeled and coarsely chopped

½ tsp salt

1 tsp ground cumin

1 tsp ground coriander

½ tsp garam masala

¼-½ tsp chili powder

¼ tsp Tandoori color or a few drops of red food coloring mixed with 1 Tbsp tomato paste

Juice of half a lemon

3 Tbsps water

2 Tbsps oil

Mix the following ingredients in a small bowl

2 heaped Tbsps all-purpose flour

½ tsp chili powder

¼ tsp salt

Wash the fish and dry on paper towels. Cut into 1-inch squares. If using frozen fish, defrost it thoroughly and dry on paper towels before cutting it. Add the salt to the ginger and garlic and crush to a smooth pulp. In a small bowl, mix together the ginger/garlic pulp, cumin, coriander, garam masala, chili powder, and Tandoori color or tomato paste mix. Add the lemon juice and water and mix thoroughly. Set aside.

Heat the oil over medium heat in a non-stick or cast iron skillet. Dust each piece of fish in the seasoned flour and put in the hot oil in a single layer, leaving plenty of room in the pan. Fry for 5 minutes, 2½ minutes each side, and drain on paper towels. Return all the fish to the pan. Hold a strainer over the pan and pour the liquid spice mixture into it. Press with the back of a metal spoon until the mixture looks dry and very coarse; discard this mixture. Stir gently and cook over medium heat until the fish is fully coated with the spices and the liquid has evaporated. Remove from the heat and serve.

Time: Preparation takes 15 minutes and cooking takes 15-20 minutes.

Serving Idea: Serve garnished with shredded lettuce leaves, sliced cucumber, and raw onion rings.

Poultry

The rise in the popularity of poultry has been phenomenal. At one time chicken was seen as a once a week treat, whereas today many of us eat far more chicken than we do beef or any other meat.

One of the most important reasons for this revolution is the widespread recognition that we need to cut down on our intake of fat. Poultry fits the criteria for a healthy source of protein perfectly: provided the skin is removed, it is a low in fat, it contains a high proportion of unsaturated fatty acids, ounce for ounce it contains more protein than red meat, and it contains a number of useful nutrients. In addition to its health benefits, poultry is a very versatile meat: it can be mixed with numerous other ingredients, it absorbs flavors well, is excellent served cold in salads, is great in stir-fries, and can be turned into the most impressive dinner party dish – the list is endless. Last, but certainly not least, is the crucial factor of time. In an age when we are all struggling to meet our commitments, most people have little time to spend on preparing meals. Poultry offers the perfect solution – it can be stir-fried, broiled or fried in a matter of minutes and to make things even faster chicken and turkey, in particular, are available in a variety of cuts such as breast, wings, quarters, and even ready-chopped for stir-frying. All of these various cuts can be put to good use if you wish to save time although, if expense is a factor, it is often more economical to buy a whole chicken and joint it yourself.

Hot and spicy recipes featuring poultry are among the most popular, as any visit to your local Mexican restaurant will confirm. Chicken features strongly in most contemporary recipe books and, although it is by far the most popular form, we mustn't forget poultry means more than just chicken. Duck, for instance, is a treat not to be overlooked. It has a flavor all its own, is perfectly complemented by a subtle mixture of spices – try Duck Breast with Spices – and offers a particularly good alternative to chicken for special occasions. Moving away from duck, why not try a whole bird such as Cornish Game Hen or Spanish Guinea Fowl; again these are perfect for impressing your guests.

The diversity of this chapter reflects the huge variety of poultry recipes available – there are spicy stir-fries from China, wonderfully refreshing chili-laden dishes from Thailand, some good old Mexican favorites, and even a few Southern classics such as Chicken Jambalaya. The key to getting the most out of chicken is to use it to its full potential, so don't be tempted to stick to what is familiar; go ahead and try a few of the more exotic recipes and you will find that cooking with poultry can be even more exciting than you imagined.

Chicken Chaat

Cubes of chicken meat, stir-fried with a light coating of spices, taste superb and look impressive served with a crisp salad.

SERVES 4

1½ pounds chicken breasts, skinned and boned
1 tsp salt or to taste
2-3 cloves garlic, coarsely chopped
2 Tbsps oil
1½ tsps ground coriander
¼ tsp turmeric
¼-½ tsp chili powder
1½ Tbsps lemon juice
2 Tbsps finely chopped fresh coriander

Wash the chicken and dry on paper towels. Cut into 1-inch cubes. Add the salt to the garlic and crush to a smooth pulp. Heat the oil in a skillet, over medium heat. Add the garlic and fry until it is lightly browned. Add the chicken and fry for 6-7 minutes until cooked, stirring constantly. Add the ground coriander, turmeric, and chili powder. Fry for 3-4 minutes, stirring frequently. Remove from heat and stir in the lemon juice and fresh coriander.

Time: Preparation takes 15 minutes and cooking takes 12-15 minutes.

Serving Idea: Serve with a garnish of crisp lettuce, sliced cucumber, sliced onions, and wedges of lemon.

Chicken Gumbo

This tasty recipe is a great favorite with kids.

SERVES 4-6

½ cup oil
3 pound chicken, cut into 6-8 pieces
1 cup all-purpose flour
2-3 dried red chilies or 1-2 fresh chilies
1 large onion, finely chopped
1 large green bell pepper, coarsely chopped
3 stalks celery, finely chopped
2 cloves garlic, finely chopped
8 oz andouille sausage or garlic sausage, diced
4 cups chicken broth
1 bay leaf
Dash of Tabasco sauce
4 oz fresh okra, trimmed and halved

Heat the oil in a large skillet and brown the chicken on both sides, 3-4 pieces at a time. Set the chicken aside. Add the flour to the pan and cook over a very low heat for about 30 minutes. Stir constantly until the flour turns a rich, dark brown. Add the chilies, onion, bell pepper, celery, garlic, and sausage to the roux and cook for about 5 minutes over very low heat, stirring continuously. Pour on the broth, and stir well. Add the bay leaf, Tabasco sauce, and salt and pepper, then bring to a boil. Reduce the heat and return the chicken to the pan. Cover and cook for about 30 minutes. Add the okra to the chicken and cook for another 10-15 minutes. Remove the bay leaf before serving.

Time: Preparation takes 30 minutes and cooking takes about 1 hour 25 minutes.

Flautas

Flautas, literally flutes, are rather elegant double length stuffed tortillas, made by filling and rolling two overlapping tortillas at once.

SERVES 6

1 Tbsp oil

8 oz chicken, skinned, boned and ground or finely chopped

1 small onion, finely chopped

½ green bell pepper, finely chopped

½–1 chili, seeded and finely chopped

3 oz frozen corn

6 black olives, pitted and chopped

½ cup heavy cream

Salt

12 prepared tortillas (see page 84)

Taco sauce (see page 67), guacamole, and sour cream for toppings

Heat the oil in a medium skillet and add the chicken, onion, and bell pepper. Cook over moderate heat, stirring frequently to break up the pieces of chicken. When the chicken is cooked and the vegetables are softened, add the chili, corn, olives, cream, and salt. Bring to a boil and boil rapidly, stirring continuously, to reduce and thicken the cream. Place 2 tortillas side by side on a clean work surface, overlapping them by about 2 inches. Spoon some of the chicken mixture in a line across the middle of the 2 tortillas, roll up the two together and secure with wooden picks. Fry each flauta in about ½ inch oil in a large sauté pan. Do not allow them to get very brown. Drain on paper towels. Arrange flautas on serving plates and top with sour cream, guacamole, and taco sauce.

Time: Preparation takes about 1 hour 25 minutes.

Serving Idea: Rice, refried beans and a tomato and avocado salad will complete this meal.

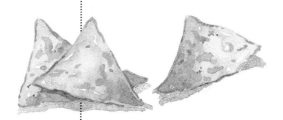

Tamarind Chicken Satay

Traditionally, satay is served as only a part of a meal, but this version is so good that it needs only a tomato and chili sambal as an accompaniment.

SERVES 4

4 chicken breasts, skinned, boned, and cut into ½-inch cubes

Marinade

1 Tbsp oil

2-inch piece tamarind, soaked in ½ cup hot water or lemon juice

2 cloves garlic, finely chopped

1 tsp ground cardamom

½ tsp ground nutmeg

Salt and freshly ground black pepper

1 tsp kecap manis (sweet soy sauce)

Tomato and chili sambal

2 red chilies

1 small piece fresh ginger root, peeled and grated

1 clove garlic, finely chopped

1 pound fresh tomatoes, peeled and seeded

4 Tbsps oil

1 Tbsp lemon or lime juice

1 Tbsp dark brown sugar

Salt and freshly ground black pepper

Put the chicken in a large bowl. Mix together the marinade ingredients and pour them over the chicken. Stir well and refrigerate for at least 30 minutes.

Grind together the chilies, ginger, and garlic in a food processor, or use a pestle and mortar. Chop the tomatoes coarsely and blend them into the chili mixture. Heat the oil in a wok or skillet and fry the tomato mixture for about 5-6 minutes, stirring occasionally to prevent it sticking. Add the lemon juice and a spoonful of water if the sauce becomes too thick. Stir in the sugar and seasoning to taste. Thread the marinated chicken cubes onto thin wooden skewers. Cook the chicken under a preheated broiler, turning frequently until golden brown – about 5-8 minutes. Brush the chicken with the remaining marinade during cooking.

Time: Preparation takes about 30 minutes and cooking takes 10-15 minutes.

Serving Idea: Serve the satay on a bed of rice with the tomato chili sambal.

Cook's Tip: If you cannot obtain tamarind use the juice of 2 lemons instead. The kecap manis may be hard to find and can be replaced by ½ teaspoon dark brown sugar and 1 teaspoon dark soy sauce.

The delightful flavor of duck mixes perfectly with the spices in this unusual recipe.

SERVES 6

3 duck breasts

5 slices fresh ginger root, peeled

2 Tbsps honey

½ tsp curry powder

½ tsp turmeric

Pinch of cinnamon

½ cup soy sauce

3 firm tomatoes

1 large zucchini

3 Tbsps olive oil

1 sprig dried thyme

1 Tbsp sugar

2 Tbsps vinegar

½ clove garlic, finely chopped

6 Tbsps water

1 Tbsp fresh chives, chopped

The day before, prepare the marinade. Chop the ginger finely. In a bowl, mix together the honey, curry powder, turmeric, cinnamon, ginger, and 3 tablespoons soy sauce. Slit the duck breasts using the point of a small knife, season on each side with salt and pepper. Brush the marinade over the duck breasts and marinate for 24 hours. Reserve the marinade.

Slice the tomatoes thinly with a serrated knife. Cut the zucchini into thin rounds with a sharp knife or a vegetable slicer. Plunge the zucchini into boiling, salted water for 1 minute. Drain and dry on paper towels. Oil squares of wax paper and interlace the tomato and zucchini slices to form a rose pattern. Season the vegetable rosettes with salt and pepper, brush lightly with olive oil and sprinkle with thyme. Just before serving, cook 10 minutes in the oven with the duck breasts.

Heat 2 tablespoons oil in a skillet and sear the duck breasts, beginning skin side down and turning after 1 minute. Finish cooking in a preheated 400°F oven for 10-15 minutes.

In a saucepan, mix together the sugar, vinegar, garlic, 5 tablespoons soy sauce, and 6 tablespoons water. Add the reserved marinade. Bring to a boil, then remove from the heat. Cut the breasts into thin slices and serve with the tomato and zucchini rosettes, and a little of the warm sauce. Garnish with chopped chives.

Time: Preparation takes 40 minutes, plus time for marinating. Cooking takes 30 minutes.

Coriander Chicken

Coriander Chicken tastes wonderful and looks very impressive.

2¼ pounds chicken joints, skinned

2-4 cloves garlic, finely chopped

⅔ cup thick set plain yogurt

5 Tbsps oil

1 large onion, finely sliced

2 Tbsps ground coriander

½ tsp ground black pepper

1 tsp ground allspice

½ tsp turmeric

½ tsp cayenne pepper or chili powder

½ cup warm water

1 tsp salt or to taste

¼ cup ground almonds

2 hard-cooked eggs, sliced

¼ tsp paprika

Mix the chicken thoroughly with the crushed garlic and yogurt, cover and marinate overnight in the refrigerator. Heat the oil and fry the onions until golden brown. Set aside. In the same oil, fry the coriander, pepper, allspice, and turmeric for 15 seconds and add the chicken and marinade. Adjust heat to medium-high and fry the chicken for 5-6 minutes. Add the cayenne or chili powder, water, salt, and the fried onion slices. Bring to a boil, cover the pan and simmer for about 30 minutes. Stir in the ground almonds and remove from heat.

Time: Preparation takes 20 minutes, plus time needed for marinating, and cooking takes 45-50 minutes.

Cornish Game Hen with – Spicy Sauce –

This recipe is perfect for entertaining.

4 Cornish game hens

1¼ tsps each of paprika, mustard powder, and ground ginger

¾ tsp turmeric

Pinch of ground allspice

5 Tbsps unsalted butter

2½ Tbsps chili sauce

1¼ Tbsps plum chutney

1¼ Tbsps brown sauce

1¼ Tbsps Worcestershire sauce

1¼ Tbsps soy sauce

Dash of Tabasco sauce

4 Tbsps chicken broth

Tie the legs of each hen together and tuck them under the wing tips. Mix the paprika, mustard, ginger, turmeric, and allspice together well and rub evenly on all sides of the birds. Refrigerate the hens for at least 1 hour.

Arrange the hens in a roasting pan. Melt the butter and brush it evenly over the birds. Roast in a preheated 350°F oven for 20 minutes, brushing with the roasting juices during this time. Put the chili sauce, plum chutney, brown sauce, Worcestershire sauce, soy sauce, Tabasco sauce and chicken broth into a bowl and mix well. Brush about half of this sauce over the birds. Return to the oven and cook for a further 40 minutes. Brush the hens twice more with the remaining sauce mixture during this time to brown the skin.

Time: Preparation takes about 25 minutes, plus 1 hour standing time. Cooking takes 60-70 minutes.

Chicken with "Burnt" Peppers

"Burning" peppers is a technique for removing the skins; it also imparts a delicious flavor to this favorite vegetable.

SERVES 4

2 red bell peppers, halved
1 green bell pepper, halved
6 Tbsps oil, for brushing
1½ Tbsps olive oil
3 tsps paprika
Pinch of ground cumin
Pinch of cayenne pepper
2 cloves garlic, finely chopped
1 pound canned tomatoes, drained and chopped
4½ Tbsps chopped fresh coriander
4½ Tbsps chopped fresh parsley
Salt, for seasoning
4 large chicken breasts, skinned and boned
1 large onion, sliced
⅓ cup slivered almonds

Put the peppers, cut side down, on a flat surface and gently press them with the palm of your hand to flatten them out. Brush the skin side with 3 tablespoons of the vegetable oil and cook them under a hot broiler until the skin chars and splits. Wrap the peppers in a clean towel for 10 minutes to cool. Unwrap the peppers and carefully peel off the charred skin. Chop the pepper flesh into thin strips.

Heat the olive oil in a skillet and gently fry the paprika, cumin, cayenne pepper, and garlic for 2 minutes, stirring to prevent the garlic from browning. Stir in the tomatoes, coriander, and parsley, and season with a little salt. Simmer for 15-20 minutes, or until thick. Set aside. Heat the remaining vegetable oil in a large pan, and sauté the chicken breasts, turning them frequently until they are golden brown on both sides. Remove the chicken and set aside. Gently fry the onions in the oil for about 5 minutes, or until softened but not overcooked. Return the chicken to the pan with the onions and pour on about 1¼ cups of water. Bring to a boil. Cover the pan and simmer for about 30 minutes, turning the chicken occasionally to prevent it from burning. Remove the chicken from the pan and boil the remaining liquid rapidly to reduce to about ⅓ cup of stock. Add the peppers and the tomato sauce to the chicken stock and stir well. Return the chicken to the pan; cover and simmer very gently for a further 30 minutes, or until the chicken is tender. Arrange the chicken on a serving dish with a little of the sauce spooned over. Sprinkle with the almonds and serve any remaining sauce separately.

Time: Preparation takes 30 minutes and cooking takes about 1 hour 30 minutes.

Duck with Sesame Seeds

If you like rare steak cook the duck breast to the same degree – it tastes really delicious. Serve with a mixed leaf salad.

SERVES 4

4 boned duck breasts

4 Tbsps sesame seeds

Marinade

4 Tbsps soy sauce

½ cup dry white wine

3 Tbsps oil

Pinch of ground nutmeg

Pinch of ground ginger

Pinch of ground mustard

Salt and pepper

Sauce

Reserved marinade

⅔ cup orange juice

1 shallot, finely chopped

2 tsps cornstarch

Garnish

1 orange, peel and white part removed, flesh thinly sliced

Brown sugar

Score the skin side of each duck breast with a sharp knife. Mix the marinade ingredients together and pour over the duck in a shallow dish. Cover and refrigerate for 2 hours, turning the duck frequently. Place the duck breasts skin side up under a medium broiler and cook for 4-7 minutes for rare duck, or 10-12 minutes for more cooked meat. Baste frequently. If the duck appears to be cooking too quickly, turn and baste more often. Combine the sauce ingredients and add any remaining marinade. Cook for 1-2 minutes over a moderate heat until boiling. Just before the duck is finished cooking, brush the skin side lightly with the sauce and sprinkle on the sesame seeds. Return the duck to the broiler for 1 minute. Serve the remaining sauce with the duck. To prepare the garnish, five minutes before the duck is cooked, sprinkle the orange slices with some brown sugar and broil on both sides to glaze. Serve with the duck.

Time: Preparation takes 15 minutes plus 2 hours marinating time. Cooking takes between 8 and 24 minutes, depending on degree of doneness required.

Preparation: Allow the duck to come to room temperature before cooking.

Sichuan Chili Chicken

If you like chilies this is sure to become a favorite.

SERVES 3-4

¾ pound chicken breast meat, cooked
1 tsp salt
1 egg white
⅓ cup oil
1½ Tbsps cornstarch
2 slices fresh ginger root, peeled
2 small dried chilies
2 green or red bell peppers
2 fresh chilies
2 Tbsps soy sauce
2 Tbsps wine vinegar

Cut the chicken into bite-sized pieces. Mix the salt, egg white, 1 tablespoon oil, and cornstarch and rub evenly over the chicken pieces to form a thin coating. Chop the ginger and dried chili. Cut the peppers into bite-sized pieces. Heat the remaining oil in a wok. Add the ginger and chilies, and stir-fry for 1 minute. Add the chicken pieces, separating them while stirring. Add the pepper, soy sauce, and vinegar, and fry for 2 minutes. Serve immediately.
Time: Preparation takes 5 minutes and cooking takes 5 minutes.

Chicken in Hot Pepper Sauce

Stir-fried chicken is served with peppers in a hot sauce in this delicous recipe.

SERVES 4

1 medium-sized chicken
2 Tbsps oil
1 tsp chopped garlic
1 green bell pepper, cut into thin strips
1 red bell pepper, cut into thin strips
1 tsp wine vinegar
1 Tbsp light soy sauce
1 tsp sugar
1⅓ cups chicken broth
1 Tbsp chili sauce
Salt and freshly ground black pepper

First, bone the chicken. To bone the legs, cut down along the bone on all sides, drawing out the bone with an even movement. Cut all the chicken meat into thin strips. Heat the oil in a wok and stir-fry the garlic, chicken, and green and red peppers for 4-5 minutes. Pour off any excess oil and deglaze the wok with the vinegar. Stir in the soy sauce, sugar, and stock. Gradually stir in the chili sauce. Season with a little salt and pepper to taste. Cook until the sauce has reduced slightly and serve immediately.
Time: Preparation takes 10 minutes and cooking takes approximately 25 minutes.
Variation: If you prefer a really hot dish, double the quantity of chili sauce.

Chicken Nueva
— Mexicana —

6 chicken thighs, skinned and boned

2 Tbsps mild chili powder

2 Tbsps oil

Juice of 1 lime

Pinch of salt

Lime cream sauce

¾ cup sour cream or plain yogurt

1 tsp lime juice and grated rind

6 Tbsps heavy cream

Salt

Corn crêpes

1 cup fine yellow cornmeal

½ cup all-purpose flour

Pinch of salt

1 whole egg and 1 egg yolk

1 Tbsp oil or melted butter or margarine

1½ cups milk

Garden salsa

1 large zucchini, diced

1 large ripe tomato, skinned and diced

2 shallots, diced

1 Tbsp chopped fresh coriander

Pinch of cayenne, freshly ground black pepper and salt

1 Tbsp white wine vinegar

3 Tbsps oil

Avocado and orange salad

2 oranges

1 avocado, peeled and sliced

Juice of 1 lime

Pinch of sugar and ground coriander

6 Tbsps pine nuts, toasted

Place the chicken in a shallow dish. Combine the chili powder, oil, lime juice, and salt, and pour over the chicken. Cover and refrigerate for 2 hours. Combine all the ingredients for the Lime Cream Sauce and fold together. Cover and chill for 2 hours.

Sift the cornmeal, flour, and salt for the crêpes into a bowl. Combine the eggs, oil, and milk. Make a well in the center of the ingredients in the bowl and pour in the liquid. Stir the liquid ingredients with a wooden spoon to gradually incorporate the dry ingredients. Leave the batter to stand for 30 minutes. Combine the salsa ingredients, cover and leave to marinate. Heat a small amount of oil in a large skillet and place in the chicken in a single layer. Fry quickly to brown both sides. Pour over remaining marinade, cover and cook until tender, about 25 minutes. Heat a small amount of oil in an 8-inch crêpe or skillet. Wipe out with paper towels and return the pan to the heat until hot. Pour a spoonful of the batter into the pan and swirl to coat the bottom with the mixture. Make sure the edge of each crêpe is irregular. When the edges of each crêpe look pale brown and the top surface begins to bubble, turn the crêpes using a palette knife. Cook the other side. Stack as each is finished. Cover with foil and keep warm in a low oven. Combine all the salad ingredients, except the pine nuts, and toss gently. To assemble, place one corn crêpe on a serving plate. Place a piece of chicken on the lower half of the crêpe, top with a spoonful of Lime Cream Sauce. Place a serving of Garden Salsa and one of Avocado and Orange Salad on either side of the chicken and partially fold the crêpe over the top. Scatter over the pine nuts.

Time: Preparation takes about 2 hours plus chilling time.

Chicken Tomato

Made with a very fragrant selection of spices, this dish is sure to become a firm favorite.

SERVES 4-6

1 medium onion, chopped
3 Tbsps oil
1 inch piece cinnamon stick
1 bay leaf
6 cloves
Seeds of 6 small cardamoms
1 inch piece fresh ginger root, peeled and grated
4 cloves garlic, finely chopped
3 pound roasting chicken, cut into 8-10 pieces
1 tsp chili powder
1 tsp ground cumin
1 tsp ground coriander
14 oz canned tomatoes, chopped
1 tsp salt
2 sprigs fresh coriander, chopped
2 green chilies, halved and seeded

Fry the onion in the oil until it has softened. Add the cinnamon, bay leaf, cloves, cardamom seeds, ginger, and garlic. Fry for 1 minute. Add the chicken pieces. Sprinkle the chili powder, ground cumin, and coriander over the chicken. Fry for a further 2 minutes, stirring continuously. Stir in the remaining ingredients, mixing well to blend the spices evenly. Cover the pan and simmer for 40-45 minutes, or until the chicken is tender.
Time: Preparation takes about 30 minutes and cooking takes about 40-50 minutes.

Brunswick Stew

Originally a squirrel stew, Brunswick stew now features chicken.

SERVES 12

2¹/₂ pounds chicken pieces
1 pound beef, diced
1¹/₂ pounds pork, diced
Seasoned all-purpose flour
6 Tbsps butter
1¹/₂ quarts tomatoes, chopped
1¹/₂ pounds potatoes
¹/₂ pound corn on the cob
³/₄ pound onions
¹/₂ pound lima beans
¹/₂ pound okra
¹/₂ pound carrots
1¹/₂ quarts water
1 pint ketchup
Salt and freshly ground black pepper

Coat all the meat lightly with seasoned flour. Heat the butter in a large skillet and brown the meat in batches. Drain the meat, and set aside. Clean and dice the potatoes, onions, okra, and carrots, but leave the lima beans and the corn on the cob whole. Place the water in an 8-quart pot and add all of the vegetables, including the tomatoes and the meat. Bring to a boil, then simmer for 1¹/₂ hours. Mix in the ketchup, stirring constantly. Cook over a medium heat for another 45 minutes. Season before serving.
Time: Preparation takes about 1 hour and cooking takes about 2 hours.

Chicken & Sausage —Jambalaya—

Jambalaya is a hearty one-pot dish.

SERVES

3 pounds chicken portions, skinned, boned, and cut into cubes (bones and skin reserved)

1 large onion, coarsely chopped

3 stalks celery, coarsely chopped

3 Tbsps butter or margarine

1 large green bell pepper, coarsely chopped

1 clove garlic, finely chopped

1 tsp each cayenne, white, and black pepper

1 cup uncooked rice

14 oz canned tomatoes

6 oz andouille (smoked pork) sausage cut into ½-inch dice

3 cups chicken stock

Chopped parsley, to garnish

Use the chicken bones and skin, and onion and celery trimmings to make broth. Cover the ingredients with water, bring to a boil and then simmer slowly for 1 hour. Strain and reserve. Melt the butter or margarine in a large saucepan and add the onion. Cook slowly to brown and then add the celery, bell pepper, and garlic; cook briefly. Add the three kinds of pepper and the rice, stirring to mix well. Add the chicken, tomatoes, sausage, and the broth. Season and mix well. Bring to a boil, then reduce the heat and simmer about 20-25 minutes, stirring occasionally until the chicken is done and the rice is tender. Garnish with chopped parsley.

Time: Preparation takes about 30 minutes and cooking takes 20-25 minutes.

Chicken Country Captain

This makes a perfect family meal.

SERVES 6

3 Tbsps oil

1½ cups chopped onions

1 clove garlic, finely chopped

¾ cup chopped green bell pepper

1 tsp curry powder

¼ tsp thyme

⅛ tsp cayenne pepper

2 Tbsps chopped fresh parsley

32 oz can tomatoes, drained and chopped

4 pound frying chicken, cut into serving-size pieces

1 cup all-purpose flour, seasoned with salt and pepper

Oil for frying

½ cup water

½ cup currants

32 whole roasted almonds

Heat the oil and sauté the onions, garlic, green pepper, and curry powder until the vegetables are tender. Add the thyme, cayenne, parsley, and tomatoes. Cover, and simmer for 1 hour. Sprinkle the chicken pieces with salt and pepper and dredge in the flour. Heat the oil to 375°F, add the chicken pieces and fry until just done – about 10-15 minutes. Place the cooked chicken in a roasting pan, add the water and sprinkle with the currants. Pour the vegetables over, cover and bake at 325°F for 1 hour. Garnish with the roasted almonds.

Time: Preparation takes about 30 minutes and cooking takes 45 minutes.

Chicken Green Chili

If you enjoy a really hot dish, leave the seeds in the chilies.

SERVES 4

Sauce
1 tsp light soy sauce
1 tsp dark soy sauce
Salt to taste
2 tsps cornstarch
1 tsp sesame oil
1 tsp malt vinegar
½ pint chicken broth

Seasoning
Salt to taste
Freshly ground black pepper to taste
2 Tbsps dark soy sauce
1 Tbsp light soy sauce
1 tsp cornstarch
2 tsps rice wine or dry sherry
1 pound boned chicken, cut into bite-size pieces
3 Tbsps oil
3 green onions, chopped
1 inch piece fresh ginger root, peeled and sliced
2 cloves garlic, sliced
1 green bell pepper, chopped
3 green chilies, sliced lengthways and seeded

Mix the sauce ingredients together and set aside. Mix the seasoning ingredients together and add the chicken. Marinate for 10 minutes. Drain the chicken and discard the liquid. Heat 1 tablespoon oil and stir-fry the onions, ginger, and garlic for 2 minutes. Remove to a dish. Add the remaining oil and stir-fry the chicken for 3 minutes. Add the green peppers and chilies and stir-fry for 2 minutes. Add the onion mixture and the well-blended sauce ingredients and cook for 3-4 minutes, until the sauce thickens. Serve immediately.

Time: Preparation takes about 20 minutes and cooking takes 10 minutes.

Spanish Guinea Fowl

The olive oil in this recipe gives a wonderful flavor to the sauce.

SERVES 4

4 small guinea fowl

Salt and freshly ground black pepper

Olive oil

4 small wedges of lime or lemon

4 bay leaves

3 Tbsps olive oil

1 small onion, thinly sliced

1 clove garlic, finely chopped

1 pound tomatoes

2/3 cup red wine

2/3 cup chicken or vegetable stock

1 1/2 Tbsps tomato paste

1 green chili, seeded and thinly sliced

1 small red bell pepper, cut into thin strips

1 small green bell pepper, cut into thin strips

3 Tbsps chopped blanched almonds

1 1/2 Tbsps pine kernels

12 small black olives, pitted

1 1/2 Tbsps raisins

Rub the guinea fowl inside and out with salt and pepper. Brush the skins with olive oil and push a wedge of lemon or lime and a bay leaf into the center of each one.

Roast the guinea fowl, uncovered, in a preheated 375°F oven for 45 minutes, or until just tender. Heat the 3 tablespoons olive oil in a large skillet and gently cook the onion and the garlic until they are soft, but not colored. Cut a slit into the skins of each tomato and plunge into boiling water for 30 seconds. Using a sharp knife, carefully peel away the skins from the blanched tomatoes. Chop the tomatoes. Remove and discard the seeds and cores. Add the chopped tomatoes to the cooked onion and garlic, and fry gently for 2 minutes. Add all the remaining ingredients and simmer for 10-15 minutes, or until the tomatoes have completely softened and the sauce has thickened slightly. Arrange the guinea fowl on a serving dish and spoon a little of the sauce over each one. Serve hot with the remaining sauce in a separate jug.

Time: Preparation takes 15 minutes and cooking takes about 1 hour.

Cook's Tip: If the guinea fowl start to get too brown during the cooking time, cover them with aluminum foil.

Chicken & Eggplant Chili

This unusual dish is both delicious and filling.

SERVES 4

2 medium eggplants
5 Tbsps sesame oil
2 cloves garlic, finely chopped
4 green onions
1 green chili, seeded and finely chopped
¾ pound boned and skinned chicken breast
5 Tbsps light soy sauce
2½ Tbsps chicken stock
1¼ Tbsps tomato paste
1 tsp cornstarch

Cut the eggplant into quarters lengthwise, using a sharp knife. Slice the eggplant quarters into pieces approximately ½-inch thick. Put the eggplant slices into a bowl and sprinkle liberally with salt. Stir well to coat evenly. Cover with plastic wrap and leave to stand for 30 minutes. Rinse the eggplant slices very thoroughly under running water, then pat dry with paper towels.

Heat half of the oil in a wok or large skillet, and gently cook the garlic until it is soft, but not colored. Add the eggplant slices to the wok and cook, stirring frequently, for 3-4 minutes. Using a sharp knife, slice the green onions into thin diagonal strips. Stir the green onions together with the chili into the cooked eggplant, and cook for 1 minute. Remove the eggplant and onion from the pan and set aside, keeping warm.

Cut the chicken breast into thin slices with a sharp knife. Heat the remaining oil in the wok, and fry the chicken pieces for approximately 2 minutes, or until they have turned white and are cooked thoroughly. Return the eggplant and onions to the pan and cook, stirring continuously, for 2 minutes or until heated through completely. Mix together the remaining ingredients and pour these over the chicken and eggplant in the wok, stirring constantly until the sauce has thickened and cleared. Serve immediately.

Time: Preparation takes about 10 minutes and cooking takes approximately 15 minutes.

Variation: Use turkey instead of chicken in this recipe, and zucchini in place of the eggplants.

Serving Idea: Serve this recipe as part of a more extensive Chinese-style meal.

Chicken Monterey

There's a touch of Mexican flavor in this chicken recipe.

6 chicken breasts, boned
Grated rind and juice of 1 lime
2 Tbsps olive oil
Coarsely ground black pepper
6 Tbsps whole grain mustard
2 tsps paprika
4 ripe tomatoes, peeled, seeded and quartered
2 shallots, chopped
1 clove garlic, finely chopped
½ red or green chili, seeded and chopped
1 tsp wine vinegar
2 Tbsps chopped fresh coriander
Whole coriander sprigs, to garnish

Place the chicken breasts in a shallow dish with the lime rind and juice, oil, pepper, mustard, and paprika. Marinate for about 1 hour, turning occasionally. Place tomatoes, shallots, garlic, chili pepper, vinegar, and salt in a food processor or blender and process until coarsely chopped. Stir in the coriander by hand. Place chicken on a broiler pan and reserve the marinade. Cook the chicken skin-side uppermost for about 7-10 minutes. Baste frequently with the remaining marinade. Broil other side in the same way. Sprinkle with a little salt after broiling. Place chicken on serving plates and garnish top with coriander sprigs. Serve with a spoonful of the tomato salsa on one side.

Time: Preparation takes about 1 hour and cooking takes 14-20 minutes.

Chicken with Chili & Basil

Fresh basil gives a wonderful flavor to this unusual, yet simple, dish.

4 chicken quarters
3 large red chilies, seeded and chopped
1 Tbsp fresh coriander root and stem, chopped
2 cloves garlic, finely chopped
3 Tbsps oil
2 green chilies, seeded and sliced
2 Tbsps fish sauce
1 Tbsp oyster sauce (optional)
Small bunch basil, torn into small pieces

Cut the chicken into smaller pieces using a large sharp knife or a meat cleaver. Pound the red chilies, coriander, and garlic together in a pestle and mortar. Heat the oil in a wok and fry the chicken until golden and almost cooked through. Remove from the pan. Add the pounded chili mixture and fry for a few minutes. Return the chicken to the pan and add the green chilies, fish sauce, and oyster sauce if using. Cook over a medium heat for 5-10 minutes or until chicken is completely cooked. Stir in the basil leaves and serve.

Time: Preparation takes 20 minutes and cooking takes 20 minutes.

Cook's Tip: Tearing basil leaves rather than cutting them with a knife allows more flavor to be released.

Chicken Moghlai with Chutney

The creamy spiciness of the chicken is a good contrast to the heat of the chutney.

SERVES 4-6

4 Tbsps oil
3 pounds chicken pieces, skinned
1 tsp ground cardamom
½ tsp ground cinnamon
1 bay leaf
4 cloves
2 onions, finely chopped
1-inch piece fresh ginger root, peeled and grated
4 cloves garlic, finely chopped
¼ cup ground almonds
2 tsps cumin seeds
Pinch of cayenne pepper
1 cup light cream
6 Tbsps plain yogurt
2 Tbsps roasted cashew nuts
2 Tbsps golden raisins
Salt

Chutney
3 oz fresh coriander
1 green chili, seeded and chopped
1 Tbsp lemon juice
Salt and freshly ground black pepper
Pinch of sugar
1 Tbsp oil
½ tsp ground coriander

Heat the oil in a large skillet, and fry the chicken pieces on each side until golden brown. Remove the chicken and set aside. Add the cardamom, cinnamon, bay leaf, and cloves to the hot oil and meat juices, and fry for 30 seconds. Stir in the onions and fry until soft but not brown. Stir the ginger, garlic, almonds, cumin, and cayenne pepper into the onions. Cook gently for 2-3 minutes, then stir in the cream. Return the chicken pieces to the pan, along with any juices. Cover and simmer gently for 30-40 minutes, or until the chicken is cooked and tender.

While the chicken is cooking, prepare the chutney. Put the fresh coriander, chili, lemon, seasoning, and sugar into a blender or food processor and work to a paste. Heat the oil and fry the ground coriander for 1 minute. Add this mixture to the processed fresh coriander and blend in thoroughly. Just before serving, stir the yogurt, cashews, and golden raisins into the chicken. Heat through just enough to plump up the golden raisins, but do not allow the mixture to boil. Serve at once with the coriander chutney.

Time: Preparation takes about 25 minutes and cooking takes 30 to 40 minutes.

Preparation: The coriander chutney can be prepared using a pestle and mortar, if a blender or food processor is not available.

Meat

As more and more people take up the challenge of following a healthy diet, the role of meat seems to be constantly under review. Many of us now eat far less of it than was once the case, choosing instead to eat fish and chicken far more often. This does not mean, however, that meat has been relegated to the junior league – it is still an important source of complete protein, as well as a rich source of minerals and trace elements, for many people.

America is renowned as a beef producer and a country of meat eaters, although it may surprise some people to learn that the early colonists, in fact, ate far more pork than beef, mainly because pigs lived off scraps and were easier to raise and feed. This situation had changed dramatically by the second half of the nineteenth century when demand for beef grew rapidly. The popularity of pork declined for a while during this time – perhaps because it was associated with a poor man's diet – only to rise again with the introduction of the leaner meat more popular today. Lamb, although abundant, has never been quite as popular as beef and pork.

Many of the world's ethnic cuisines do not feature meat as strongly as our own does – for economical, as well as religious reasons. The plethora of meat recipes in many Ethnic restaurants over here simply reflects demand, and as we choose to eat less meat we may well see meat used in a way that is more appealing to the health-conscious and a truer reflection of these cuisines. The rise in popularity of Chinese stir-fry recipes perhaps reflects this, as the quantity of meat can be reduced in relation to the amount of vegetables, without affecting the quality and flavor of the final result.

Not all hot and spicy cuisines, of course, regard meat in the same way. In Mexican cooking meat holds much the same position as it does in the U.S. and tends to be served often as the main feature of a meal. Here, cattle were particularly popular after their introduction by the Spanish, and Mexican pork is renowned for its succulence. This is reflected in the number of delicious beef and pork recipes that grace the menus in many Mexican restaurants, although today they will now be offered alongside a wide variety of salads and vegetable dishes. Pork with Lime and Chilies, and Leg of Lamb with Chili Sauce are just two examples of recipes featured in this chapter from Mexico's exciting cuisine.

Despite the fact that meat consumption is in decline, it seems highly unlikely that we will ever become a nation of vegetarians: America is still famous for its meat and most of us still enjoy it, albeit only once or twice a week.

Penne with Spicy Chili Sauce

If you enjoy a fiery flavor, increase the amount of chilies in this recipe.

SERVES 4-6

1 pound canned tomatoes
1 Tbsp olive oil
2 cloves garlic, finely chopped
1 onion, chopped
4 strips bacon, chopped
2 red chilies, seeded and chopped
2 green onions, chopped
¼ cup grated pecorino or Parmesan cheese
1 pound penne or macaroni
Salt and freshly ground black pepper

Chop the tomatoes and sieve them to remove the pips. Heat the oil in a skillet and fry the garlic, onion, and bacon gently for 6-8 minutes. Add the sieved tomatoes, chilies, chopped green onions, and half of the cheese. Simmer gently for 20 minutes. Season to taste. Cook the penne or macaroni in boiling water for 10-15 minutes, or until tender. Rinse under hot water and drain well. Put the cooked penne into a warm serving dish and toss them in half of the sauce. Pour the remaining sauce over the top and sprinkle with the remaining cheese.

Time: Preparation takes about 15 minutes and cooking takes about 30 minutes.

Variation: Substitute 2 oz chopped mushrooms for the bacon.

Spiced Pork

Five spice is a ready-prepared spicy powder which can easily be obtained from most supermarkets. It is used in this dish with ginger and pepper to make a typical Sichuan meal.

SERVES 4

1 pound pork tenderloin
5 Tbsps sesame oil
1-inch piece fresh ginger root, peeled and chopped
1¼ tsps black peppercorns
1¼ tsps five spice powder
¼ cup dry sherry
⅔ cup light broth
3 Tbsps honey
4 green onions, sliced diagonally
½ cup bamboo shoots, shredded
1 large ripe mango, peeled and sliced

Using a sharp knife, finely slice the pork into thin strips. Put the oil into a wok or large skillet, and heat gently. Add the ginger and fry quickly for 20-30 seconds. Add the sliced meat to the wok and stir-fry for 4-5 minutes, or until the meat is well cooked and tender.

Stir the peppercorns, five spice powder, sherry, broth, and honey into the meat. Mix well and bring to a boil. Add all the remaining ingredients to the wok and cook quickly, stirring continuously for 3 minutes. Serve immediately.

Time: Preparation takes 25 minutes and cooking takes about 10 minutes.

Serving Idea: Serve with rice or Chinese noodles.

Tacos

This is a classic Tex-Mex favorite that is easily made with packaged taco shells.

SERVES 4

8 taco shells

Filling
1 Tbsp oil
1 pound ground beef
1 medium onion, chopped
2 tsps ground cumin
1 clove garlic, finely chopped
2 tsps chili powder
Pinch of paprika
Salt and freshly ground black pepper

Toppings
Shredded lettuce
Shredded cheese
Tomatoes, seeded and chopped
Chopped green onions
Avocado slices
Sour cream
Jalapeño peppers

Taco sauce

1 Tbsp oil	½ tsp ground coriander
1 onion, diced	½ clove garlic, finely chopped
1 green bell pepper, diced	Pinch of salt, black pepper and sugar
½-1 red or green chili	14 oz canned tomatoes
½ tsp ground cumin	Tomato paste (optional)

Heat the oil for filling in a large skillet and brown the beef and onion, breaking the meat up with a fork as it cooks. Add spices, garlic, and seasoning and cook about 20 minutes.

While the filling is cooking, prepare the taco sauce. Heat the oil in a heavy-bottomed saucepan and when hot, add the onion and bell pepper. Cook slowly to soften slightly. Chop the chili and add to the sauce with the cumin, coriander and garlic. Cook a further 2-3 minutes. Add sugar, seasonings, and tomatoes with their juice. Break up the tomatoes with a fork or a potato masher. Cook a further 5-6 minutes over moderate heat to reduce and thicken slightly. Add tomato paste for color, if necessary. Keep the sauce warm while preparing the taco shells.

Heat the taco shells on a cookie sheet in a preheated 350°F oven for 2-3 minutes. Place on the sheet with the open ends down. To fill, hold the shell in one hand, and spoon in about 1 tablespoon of beef filling. Next, add a layer of shredded lettuce, followed by a layer of shredded cheese. Add your choice of other toppings and finally spoon on some taco sauce.

Time: Preparation takes about 15 minutes and cooking takes about 25 minutes.

Chinese Meatballs

A slightly sweet sauce enhances the meat in this exciting recipe.

SERVES 4

¾ cup blanched almonds

1 pound ground beef

1¼ tsps grated fresh ginger root

1 clove garlic, finely chopped

½ large green bell pepper, seeded and chopped

Dash of Sichuan, chili, or Tabasco sauce

2½ Tbsps soy sauce

Oil for frying

3¾ Tbsps soy sauce

¼ cup vegetable broth

1¼ Tbsps rice wine or white wine vinegar

2½ tsps honey

1¼ Tbsps sherry

1¼ Tbsps cornstarch

4 green onions, sliced diagonally

Spread the almonds evenly onto a broiler pan, and broil under a low heat for 3-4 minutes, or until lightly toasted. Stir the almonds often to prevent them from burning. Chop the almonds coarsely using a large sharp knife. In a large bowl, combine the chopped almonds with the meat, ginger, garlic, green pepper, Sichuan sauce, and the 2½ tablespoons of soy sauce. Use a wooden spoon or your hands to ensure that the ingredients are well blended. Divide the mixture into 16 and roll each piece into small meatballs on a lightly floured board.

Heat a little oil in a large skillet and add about half of the meatballs in a single layer. Cook the meatballs over a low heat for about 20 minutes, turning them frequently until they are well browned all over. Transfer to a serving dish and keep warm while you cook the remaining meatballs. Set aside as before. Stir the 3¾ tablespoons soy sauce, broth and vinegar into the skillet and bring to a boil. Boil briskly for about 30 seconds. Add the honey and stir until dissolved. Blend the sherry and cornstarch together in a small bowl, and add this into the hot sauce. Cook, stirring all the time, until thickened. Arrange the meatballs on a serving dish and sprinkle with the sliced green onions. Pour the sauce over, and serve.

Time: Preparation takes about 20 minutes and cooking takes 40 minutes.

Freezing: The meatballs will freeze uncooked for up to 3 months. The sauce should be prepared freshly when required.

Spicy Sausages with -Peas & Mint-

Spicy sausages are a perfect foil for the mild flavor of peas and the cooling tang of mint in this informal dish.

SERVES 4-6

4 chorizos
4 oz bacon, finely diced
1 small onion, finely chopped
½ clove garlic, finely chopped
¾ cup white wine
¼ cup water
1 bay leaf
Salt and freshly ground black pepper
2 tsps chopped fresh mint
1 pound fresh peas

Place the sausages in a saucepan and add enough water to cover completely. Bring to a boil and then reduce the heat to simmering. Cook, uncovered, for about 5 minutes and drain on paper towels. Set the sausages aside.

Cook the bacon in a skillet until crisp and golden brown. Place on paper towels to drain. Add the onion and garlic to the pan and cook until the onions are softened but not browned. Add the wine, water, bay leaf, bacon, mint, salt, and pepper. Bring to a boil over high heat and then reduce to simmering. Add the sausages and peas, and cook, partially covered, for about 20 minutes. Remove sausages and slice. Add to the peas and re-heat if necessary.

Time: Preparation takes about 20 minutes and cooking takes about 35 minutes.

Spare Ribs in Chili -Cream Sauce-

Cocoa and chilies seem unlikely partners, but the combination is borrowed from Mexico where the bitter cocoa bean has been used for centuries as a valued spice that adds color, depth, and flavor.

SERVES 4

2¼ pounds spare ribs
1 tsp unsweetened cocoa
1 Tbsp all-purpose flour
½ tsp cumin
½ tsp chili powder
½ tsp dried oregano, crushed
Salt and freshly ground black pepper
1 cup warm water
2 Tbsps thin honey
2 Tbsps heavy cream
Lime wedges and watercress for garnish

Leave the ribs in whole slabs, put in a roasting pan and cook in a 400°F oven for 20-25 minutes, or until well browned. Drain off all the excess fat. Blend the cocoa, flour, cumin, chili powder, oregano, seasoning, water and honey, and pour over the ribs for a further 30 minutes, until the sauce has reduced and the ribs are tender. Cut the ribs into pieces and arrange on a serving dish. Pour the cream into the sauce in the roasting pan and place over moderate heat. Bring to a boil and pour over the ribs. Garnish with lime wedges and watercress.

Time: Preparation takes 20 minutes and cooking takes about 55 minutes.

Spiced Lamb

Lamb absorbs flavors well, and the final result of this recipe is particularly delicious.

SERVES 4

1 pound lamb neck fillets
1 tsp each chopped, fresh dill and thyme
1 tsp rosemary, crushed
2 bay leaves
2 tsps mustard seeds, lightly crushed
½ tsp ground allspice
1 tsp coarsely ground black pepper
Juice of 2 lemons
1 cup red wine
2 Tbsps oil
1 small red bell pepper, sliced
3 oz button mushrooms, left whole
2 Tbsps butter or margarine
3 Tbsps all-purpose flour
½ cup beef stock

Place the lamb in a shallow dish and sprinkle on the herbs, spices, pepper, lemon juice, and wine, and stir to coat the meat thoroughly. Leave for 4 hours in the refrigerator. Heat the oil in a large skillet, and add the bell pepper and mushrooms; cook to soften slightly. Remove with a draining spoon. Drain and dry the lamb, reserving the marinade. Add the meat to the pan and brown quickly on all sides. Remove from the pan and set aside with the vegetables. Melt the butter in the pan and, when foaming, add the flour. Lower the heat and cook the flour slowly until a good, rich brown. Stir in the broth and marinade. Bring to a boil, season and return the vegetables and lamb to the pan. Cook about 15 minutes, or until the lamb is tender, but still pink inside. Slice the lamb thinly on the diagonal and arrange on plates. Remove the bay leaves from the sauce and spoon the sauce over the meat.

Time: Preparation takes about 20 minutes, plus marinating time. Cooking takes about 35 minutes.

Chili con Carne

This is the basic Tex-Mex chili recipe – of which there are many versions and about which there are many arguments to be had! Many cooks say no beans, others dispute over the type and quality of meat used, and of course the amount of chili powder used depends on your sense of bravado.

SERVES 4

1 Tbsp oil
1 pound ground beef
2 tsps ground cumin
2 tsps chili powder
Pinch of oregano
Salt, black pepper and pinch of sugar
¼ tsp garlic powder
2 Tbsps all-purpose flour
1 pound canned tomatoes
1 pound canned red kidney beans

Heat the oil in a large skillet and brown the meat, breaking it up with a fork as it cooks. Sprinkle on the cumin, chili powder, oregano, salt, pepper, sugar, garlic, and flour. Cook, stirring frequently, over medium heat for about 3 minutes. Add the tomatoes and their liquid and simmer 25-30 minutes. Drain the kidney beans and add just before serving. Heat through for about 5 minutes.

Time: Preparation takes 15 minutes and cooking takes about 40 minutes.

Serving Idea: Top with sour cream, chopped onions, grated cheese, and diced avocado, or a combination of the four ingredients.

American Hot Pizza

The perfect hot and spicy pizza!

MAKES ONE 10-INCH PIZZA

10-inch thin-crust pizza base
¼ cup butter
1 cup mushrooms, sliced
Full quantity Tomato Sauce (see page 74)
2 green chilies, cut into rings
2 oz pepperoni, sliced
4 oz Mozzarella cheese, sliced

Melt the butter in a small saucepan and sauté the mushrooms for 2-3 minutes or until softened. Spread the tomato sauce over the pizza base, then cover with the sautéed mushrooms. Scatter half the chilies over the mushrooms, then top with a layer of pepperoni. Lay the cheese on top and scatter with the remaining chilies. Bake in a preheated 400°F oven for 10-15 minutes, or until the base is cooked and golden and the cheese has melted.

Time: Preparation takes about 25 minutes and cooking takes 15-20 minutes.

Serving Idea: A mixed leaf salad and coleslaw complement this pizza perfectly.

Beef with Peppers & Chili

The classic mix of beef and green bell pepper is given extra punch by the addition of chilies.

SERVES 4

1 pound fillet of beef, cut into 1-inch strips

Seasoning

2 Tbsps dark soy sauce

1 tsp sesame oil

Pinch of baking soda

¼ tsp ground black pepper

½ tsp salt

Oil for cooking

2 green bell peppers, thinly sliced

1 medium onion, sliced

2 green onions, chopped

1 inch fresh ginger root, peeled and chopped

2 garlic cloves, chopped

3 green chilies, seeded and sliced

Sauce

2 Tbsps chicken broth

1 tsp dark soy sauce

Salt

Few drops of sesame oil

Marinate the beef in the seasoning ingredients for 15 minutes. Heat 2 tablespoons oil in a wok and stir-fry the green pepper and onions for 2 minutes. Remove to a plate.

Reheat wok, add 2-3 tablespoons oil and fry the ginger, garlic, and green chilies for 1 minute.

Add the beef and stir-fry for 4-5 minutes. Add the sauce ingredients, mixed together, and the fried peppers and onions. Stir-fry for 2 minutes and serve.

Time: Preparation takes 30 minutes and cooking takes 10-12 minutes.

Barbecued Steak

Steak is ideal for slow grilling on a barbecue.

SERVES 6

3½ pounds steak in one piece

Barbecue sauce

4 Tbsps oil

1½ cups tomato ketchup

3 Tbsps Worcestershire sauce

6 Tbsps cider vinegar

4 Tbsps soft brown sugar

4 Tbsps chopped onion

1 clove garlic, finely chopped

1 bay leaf

4 Tbsps water

2 tsps mustard powder

Dash of Tabasco sauce

Salt and pepper

Barbecue seasoning

5 tsps salt

½ tsp freshly ground black pepper

½ tsp cayenne pepper

Combine all the ingredients for the barbecue sauce in a heavy saucepan. Reserve the salt and pepper to add later. Cook over a low heat for 30 minutes, stirring frequently and adding more water if the sauce reduces too quickly. Remove the bay leaf and add salt and pepper to taste before using. The sauce should be thick.

Score the meat across both sides with a large knife in a lattice pattern. Mix together the barbecue seasoning and rub over the meat. Sear the meat on both sides over hot coals. Raise the grill rack, to lower the temperature, baste with the sauce and grill the meat slowly. During the last 5 minutes, lower the rack to raise the temperature and grill the meat quickly on both sides, basting with the sauce. Slice the meat thinly across the grain and serve with any remaining sauce.

Time: Preparation takes about 25 minutes and cooking takes 45-55 minutes.

Spicy Beef Pizza

Add some fresh chopped chilies for a really hot pizza.

MAKES ONE 10-INCH PIZZA

Tomato sauce
1 Tbsp olive oil
1 small onion, finely chopped
1 clove garlic, finely chopped
8 oz can chopped tomatoes
½ tsp dried mixed herbs

10-inch thin-crust pizza base
6 oz lean ground beef
½ small onion, finely chopped
1 clove garlic, finely chopped
1 tsp ground allspice
1 tsp ground chili powder
½ red bell pepper and ½ green bell pepper, chopped
3 oz Cheddar cheese, grated

Heat the oil in a pan and fry the onion for 4 minutes, until beginning to soften. Stir in the garlic and fry for 1 minute. Add the tomatoes and herbs and bring to a boil. Reduce the heat and simmer gently for 10-15 minutes. Keep warm until required.

Mix the beef, onion, garlic, allspice, and chili in a bowl until well combined. Shape into 18 balls, and shallow fry in oil for about 5 minutes until browned on all sides. Place the meatballs on top of the pizza base and scatter with the chopped pepper. Spoon the tomato sauce over the pizza, sprinkle with the cheese and bake in a preheated 400°F for 15-20 minutes.
Time: Preparation takes 20 minutes, cooking takes 25 minutes.

Shredded Beef with —Vegetables—

This classic Chinese stir-fry is quick and easy to cook.

SERVES 4

8 oz steak, cut into thin strips
½ tsp salt
4 Tbsps oil
1 red and 1 green chili, seeded and sliced into strips
1 tsp vinegar
1 stalk celery, cut into 2-inch strips
2 carrots, cut into 2-inch strips
1 leek, white part only, sliced into 2-inch strips
2 cloves garlic, finely chopped
2 tsps dark soy sauce
2 tsps Chinese wine, or dry sherry
1 tsp superfine sugar
½ tsp freshly ground black pepper

Put the strips of beef into a large bowl and sprinkle with the salt. Rub the salt into the meat and allow to stand for 5 minutes. Heat 1 tablespoon of the oil in a large wok. When the oil begins to smoke, reduce the heat and stir in the beef and chilies. Stir-fry for 4-5 minutes. Add the remaining oil and continue stir-frying the beef until it turns crispy. Add the vinegar and stir until it evaporates, then add the celery, carrots, leek, and garlic. Stir-fry for 2 minutes. Mix together the soy sauces, wine or sherry, sugar, and pepper. Pour this mixture over the beef and cook for 2 minutes. Serve immediately.
Time: Preparation takes about 15 minutes and cooking takes about 10 minutes.

Pork with Lime & Chili

In this recipe, creamy coconut and fragrant spices blend together to complement the pork beautifully.

SERVES 4

1 clove garlic, finely chopped
1 tsp brown sugar
1 tsp oil
1 tsp lime juice
1 tsp cornstarch
1 pound pork tenderloin, cut into 1-inch cubes
½ cup oil, for deep frying
1 green chili, seeded and thinly sliced
1 red chili, seeded and thinly sliced
8 green onions, sliced diagonally
1 tsp turmeric
1 tsp ground coriander
1 tsp ground cumin
1 tsp ground nutmeg
Pinch of ground cloves
4 Tbsps soy sauce
Juice and rind of 1 lime
½ cup coconut milk
Salt and freshly ground black pepper

Combine the garlic, sugar, oil, lime juice, and cornstarch in a large bowl. Stir in the pork and coat thoroughly with the garlic and lime juice mixture. Allow to stand in the refrigerator for at least 1 hour.

Heat the oil in a wok and add the pork cubes. Cook, stirring frequently, for about 10 minutes until golden brown and cooked through. Drain and set aside. Remove all except about 1 tablespoon of the oil. Reheat and add the chilies and onions. Stir-fry for about 2 minutes.

Add the ground spices and fry for a further 30 seconds. Stir in the remaining ingredients and bring to a boil. Add the fried pork to the sauce and heat through. Adjust the seasoning and serve.

Time: Preparation takes about 20 minutes, plus at least 1 hour marinating. Cooking takes about 20 minutes.

Cook's Tip: If you don't have any fresh coconut milk, dissolve 1 oz creamed coconut in ½ cup hot water and use that.

Beef & Leek Skewers

An unusual combination, these kebabs are nutritious, as well as being very tasty.

1 Tbsps superfine sugar

2 Tbsps tamarind extract

1 Tbsp grated fresh ginger root

½ cup light soy sauce

Black pepper

1 pound rump steak

4 leeks

3 Tbsps oil

In a large bowl, mix together the sugar, tamarind extract, ginger, soy sauce, and pepper. Cut the steak into 1-inch cubes. Trim the leeks to leave only the white and pale green parts and cut these into 1-inch pieces. Put the beef and leeks into the marinade mixture and mix together thoroughly to coat evenly. Allow to stand for 30 minutes. Thread the beef and leeks alternately onto thin wooden kebab skewers.

Heat the oil in large skillet. Cook the kebabs in the oil, turning frequently to prevent them burning. Add the marinade mixture to the pan and cook quickly, until it has reduced to a thick syrup. Coat the kebabs with the marinade syrup before serving.

Time: Preparation takes about 15 minutes, plus standing time of 30 minutes. Cooking takes about 10 minutes.

Preparation: If tamarind extract is not available, use 2 tablespoons lemon juice.

Barbecued Pork Stew

Bell peppers, chili powder, and Tabasco sauce turn this pork stew into a really spicy dish.

SERVES 4

2 pounds pork shoulder, cut into 2-inch cubes

2 medium onions, cut into 2-inch pieces

1 large green bell pepper, cut into 2-inch pieces

1 Tbsp chili powder

2 cloves garlic, finely chopped

1 pound canned tomatoes

3 Tbsps tomato paste

1 Tbsp Worcestershire sauce

½ cup water or beef broth

2½ Tbsps cider vinegar

1 bay leaf

½ tsp dried oregano

Tabasco sauce and salt

Brown the pork in a little oil over high heat for about 5 minutes. Remove to a plate. Cook the onions and peppers to soften slightly. Add the chili powder and garlic and cook 1 minute. Add the tomatoes, their juice, and the tomato paste. Stir in the Worcestershire sauce, water or broth, and vinegar. Add bay leaf, oregano, and salt. Transfer to a flameproof casserole dish. Bring the mixture to a boil, cover, and then cook slowly for about 1½ hours. When the meat is tender, remove the bay leaf and add a few drops of Tabasco sauce and salt to taste.

Time: Preparation takes about 25 minutes and cooking takes 1½ hours.

Rogan Josh

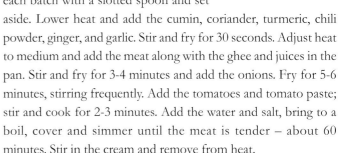

Rogan Josh finds its origin in Kashmir, the northern-most state in India. In this recipe, more than the usual quantity of spices are used, but these are toned down by using a large quantity of tomatoes and a little heavy cream.

SERVES 4-6

3 Tbsps unsalted butter

2¼ pound leg of lamb, without bones, cut into 1½-inch cubes

1 Tbsp ground cumin

1 Tbsp ground coriander

1 tsp turmeric

1 tsp chili powder

1-inch cube of ginger root, peeled and grated

2-4 cloves garlic, finely chopped

1 large onion, finely sliced

14 oz can tomatoes

1 Tbsp tomato paste

½ cup warm water

1¼ tsps salt or to taste

½ cup heavy cream

2 tsps garam masala

2 Tbsps chopped fresh coriander

Melt 2 tablespoons butter, from the specified amount, over medium heat and fry the meat in 2-3 batches until it changes color. Remove each batch with a slotted spoon and set aside. Lower heat and add the cumin, coriander, turmeric, chili powder, ginger, and garlic. Stir and fry for 30 seconds. Adjust heat to medium and add the meat along with the ghee and juices in the pan. Stir and fry for 3-4 minutes and add the onions. Fry for 5-6 minutes, stirring frequently. Add the tomatoes and tomato paste; stir and cook for 2-3 minutes. Add the water and salt, bring to a boil, cover and simmer until the meat is tender – about 60 minutes. Stir in the cream and remove from heat.

In a separate pan melt the remaining butter over medium heat and add the garam masala; stir briskly and add to the meat. Transfer a little sauce to the pan in which the garam masala was fried – stir thoroughly to ensure that any remaining garam masala and butter mixture is fully incorporated and add this to the meat. Mix well, stir in the fresh coriander, and serve.

Time: Preparation takes 20 minutes and cooking takes 1 hour 30 minutes.

Variation: Use chuck steak, but increase cooking time.

Albondigas

Taco sauce on these spicy meatballs gives this dish a double dose of flavor.

SERVES 4

8 oz ground veal

8 oz ground beef

1 clove garlic, finely chopped

2 Tbsps dry bread crumbs

½ chili, seeded and finely chopped

½ tsp ground cumin

Salt

1 egg, beaten

All-purpose flour, to coat

Oil for frying

Full quantity Taco Sauce recipe (see page 67)

2 green onions, chopped

Mix together the veal, beef, garlic, bread crumbs, chili, cumin, salt, and egg until well blended. Add the egg gradually. Turn the mixture out onto a floured surface and divide into 16 equal pieces. With floured hands, shape the mixture into balls. Pour about 3 tablespoons of oil into a large skillet and place over high heat. When the oil is hot, add the meatballs and fry for 5-10 minutes, or until brown on all sides. Turn frequently during cooking. Remove the meatballs and drain well on paper towels. Place in an ovenproof dish and pour over the taco sauce. Heat in a preheated 350°F oven for 10 minutes. Sprinkle with chopped green onions to serve.

Time: Preparation takes about 25 minutes and cooking takes 20 minutes.

Chili Verde

This pork and chickpea stew is a delicious variation on traditional chili.

SERVES 6-8

Oil

2 pounds lean pork, cut into 1-inch pieces

3 green bell peppers, cut into 1-inch pieces

1-2 green chilies, seeded and finely chopped

1 small bunch green onions, chopped

2 cloves garlic, finely chopped

2 tsps ground cumin

2 tsps chopped fresh oregano

3 Tbsps chopped fresh coriander

1 bay leaf

3 cups beer, water or chicken broth

8 oz canned chickpeas, drained

Salt

1 large ripe avocado, peeled and diced

1 Tbsp lime juice

Heat 4 tablespoons of oil in a large pan and lightly brown the pork cubes over high heat. Lower the heat, add the bell peppers and cook to soften slightly. Add the chilies, onions, garlic, and cumin, and cook for 2 minutes. Add the herbs and liquid and reduce the heat. Simmer, covered, 1-1½ hours or until the meat is tender. Add the chickpeas during the last 45 minutes. Add salt to taste and remove the bay leaf. Toss the avocado in lime juice and sprinkle over the top of the chili to serve.

Time: Preparation takes 30 minutes and cooking takes 1-1½ hours.

Indian Bread with Chorizo

A version of this bread recipe has been baked by Native Americans for hundreds of years.

SERVES 4-6

Bread
2 cups all-purpose flour

1 Tbsp baking powder

Pinch of salt

1 Tbsp vegetable shortening

2 tsps cumin seed

¾ cup plus 2 Tbsps water

Chorizo topping
1 pound cooked chorizo sausage

2 medium red potatoes, scrubbed

4 green onions, chopped

Salsa
1 clove garlic

1 oz fresh coriander

1 tsp fresh oregano

Red or green chili, seeded

Pinch of salt and dry mustard

Juice of 2 limes

¼ cup oil

Shredded lettuce, crumbled goat's milk cheese and chopped tomatoes to garnish

Sift the flour, baking powder, and salt into a bowl. Cut in the shortening until the mixture resembles coarse crumbs and then stir in the cumin seed. Stir in enough water to make a soft, slightly sticky dough. Knead several times, cover and leave to stand for 15-20 minutes. Divide the dough into 8 pieces and roll or pat into 5-inch circles on a well-floured surface. Make a hole in the center of each with your finger and leave the circles to stand, covered, for 30 minutes.

Meanwhile, boil the potatoes in their skins in a covered saucepan until tender; drain and cool, and cut into ½-inch dice. Remove the casing from the chorizo. Chop sausage coarsely and set aside. Place the garlic, coriander, oregano, chili, salt, and mustard into a food processor and add the lime juice. Process until well blended, then add the oil through the funnel in a thin, steady stream. Process until smooth and adjust the seasoning.

Heat the oil to 375°F. Carefully lower in one dough circle and push it underneath the oil with a large metal spoon. Fry for about 30 seconds, turn over and fry the other side. Drain each while frying the others. Mix the chorizo, green onions, and potatoes with enough of the salsa to moisten. Arrange the shredded lettuce on top of the bread and spoon on the chorizo topping. Spoon on any remaining salsa and sprinkle with chopped tomato and crumbled cheese.

Time: Preparation takes about 45-60 minutes and cooking takes about 10 minutes in total.

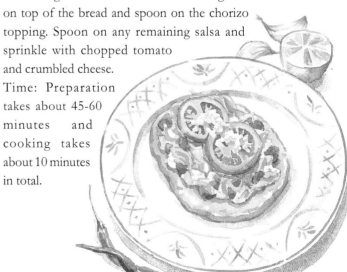

Meat Madras

This delicious curry is named after Madras, the major city in southern India, perhaps because in the humid south people eat rather hot food. Strange though it may seem, the hotter the food you eat, the cooler you feel.

SERVES 4-6

½ cup oil

2 medium onions, coarsely chopped

1-inch cube fresh ginger root, peeled and coarsely chopped

3-4 cloves garlic, coarsely chopped

4-6 dried red chilies

2 large cloves garlic, finely chopped

1-2 green chilies, sliced lengthwise

1 small can of tomatoes

3 tsps ground cumin

1 tsp ground coriander

½-1 tsp chili powder

1 tsp turmeric

2¼ pound leg or shoulder of lamb, fat removed and cut into 1½-inch cubes

¾ cup warm water

1½ tsps salt or to taste

1 tsp garam masala

Heat 3 tablespoons oil from the specified amount over medium heat and fry the onions, coarsely chopped ginger, garlic, and red chilies until the onions are soft – about 8-10 minutes – stirring frequently. Remove from heat and allow to cool.

Meanwhile, heat the remaining oil over medium heat and fry the finely chopped garlic and green chilies until garlic is lightly browned. Add half the tomatoes, along with the juice; stir and cook for 1-2 minutes. Add the cumin, coriander, chili powder, and turmeric, adjust heat to low and cook for 6-8 minutes, stirring frequently. Add the meat and adjust heat to medium-high. Stir and fry until meat changes color – 5-6 minutes. Add the water, bring to a boil, cover and simmer for 30 minutes.

Place the fried onion mixture in a blender or food processor and add the remaining tomatoes. Blend until smooth and add this to the meat, bring to a boil, add salt and mix well. Cover the pan and simmer for a further 35-40 minutes or until the meat is tender. Stir in the garam masala and remove from heat.

Time: Preparation takes 25-30 minutes, cooking takes 1 hour 20 minutes.

Southwestern Stir-fry

East meets West in this tasty dish.

SERVES 4

1 pound sirloin or rump steak	1 Tbsp ground cumin
2 cloves garlic, finely chopped	1 small red bell pepper, sliced
6 Tbsps wine vinegar	1 small green bell pepper, sliced
Pinch of sugar, salt and black pepper	2 oz baby corn
6 Tbsps oil	4 green onions, shredded
1 bay leaf	Oil for frying

Red sauce

4 Tbsps oil

1 medium onion, finely chopped

1-2 green chilies, seeded and finely chopped

1-2 cloves garlic, finely chopped

8 fresh ripe tomatoes, peeled, seeded and chopped

6 sprigs fresh coriander

3 Tbsps tomato paste

Slice the meat thinly. Combine in a plastic bag with the next 6 ingredients. Tie the bag and toss the ingredients inside to coat. Leave about 4 hours. Heat the oil for the sauce and cook the onion, chilies and garlic to soften. Add remaining sauce ingredients and cook about 15 minutes over gentle heat. Purée in a food processor until smooth. Heat a skillet and add the meat, discarding the marinade. Cook until browned and set aside. Now fry the bell peppers about 2 minutes. Add the corn and onions and return the meat to the pan. Cook another minute and add the sauce. Heat through and serve immediately.

Time: Preparation takes about 25 minutes, plus time for marinating. Cooking takes 30 minutes.

Mexican Kebabs

These delicious kebabs marry Texan barbecue cooking with the ancient spice combination of bitter cocoa and biting chilies.

SERVES 4

1 pound pork or lamb, cut into 2-inch pieces

4 oz large button mushrooms, left whole

8 bay leaves

1 tsp unsweetened cocoa

2 tsps chili powder

¼ tsp garlic powder

½ tsp dried marjoram

Salt and freshly ground black pepper

6 Tbsps oil

2 medium onions, quartered

6 oz cooked rice, to serve

½ quantity Taco Sauce recipe (see page 67)

Place meat and mushrooms in a bowl. Add the bay leaves, cocoa, chili powder, garlic powder, marjoram, and seasoning to the oil and stir into the meat and mushrooms. Cover the bowl and leave to marinate at least 6 hours, preferably overnight. Remove meat, mushrooms, and bay leaves from the marinade and reserve it. Thread onto skewers, alternating meat, onions, mushrooms, and bay leaves. Place under a preheated broiler for 15-20 minutes, turning frequently. Baste with reserved marinade. Mix hot rice with taco sauce and spoon onto a warm serving dish. Place the kebabs on top of the rice to serve.

Time: Preparation takes about 15 minutes, plus time for marinating. Cooking takes 25-30 minutes in total.

Lamb with Chili Sauce

Here familiar Tex-Mex spices – cayenne, chili, cumin, paprika – are mixed with cocoa, which is used not as a sweetening but as a seasoning as was traditional in pre-Columbian Mexico.

SERVES 4

2¼ pound leg of lamb

Marinade

1 tsp unsweetened cocoa

¼ tsp cayenne pepper

½ tsp chili powder

½ tsp ground cumin

½ tsp paprika

½ tsp ground oregano

½ cup water

½ cup orange juice

½ cup red wine

1 clove garlic, finely chopped

2 Tbsps light brown sugar

Pinch of salt

1 Tbsp cornstarch

Orange slices and coriander, to garnish

If the lamb has a lot of surface fat, trim with a sharp knife. If possible, remove the paper-thin skin on the outside of the lamb. Place lamb in a shallow dish. Mix together the marinade ingredients, except cornstarch, and pour over the lamb, turning it well to coat completely. Cover and refrigerate for 12-24 hours, turning occasionally.

Drain the lamb, reserving the marinade, and place in a roasting pan. Cook in a preheated 350°F oven for about 2 hours until meat is cooked according to taste. Baste occasionally with the marinade and pan juices. Remove lamb to a serving dish and keep warm. Skim the fat from the top of the roasting pan with a large spoon and discard. Pour remaining marinade into the pan juices in the roasting pan and bring to a boil, stirring to loosen the sediment. Mix cornstarch with a small amount of water and add some of the liquid from the roasting pan. Gradually stir cornstarch mixture into the pan and bring back to a boil. Cook, stirring constantly, until thickened and clear. Add more orange juice, wine or water as necessary. Garnish the lamb with orange slices and sprigs of coriander. Pour over some of the sauce and serve the remaining sauce separately. Time: Preparation takes about 15 minutes, plus time for marinating. Cooking takes 2 hours.

Lamb Korma

One of the best-known Indian curries, a korma is rich, spicy and a traditional favorite.

SERVES 4

3 Tbsps oil

1 medium onion, sliced

1-inch piece cinnamon stick

6 cloves

Seeds of 6 small cardamoms

1 bay leaf

1 tsp black cumin seeds

2 tsps grated fresh ginger root

2 cloves garlic, finely chopped

1 pound shoulder of lamb, cubed

1 tsp chili powder

1 tsp ground coriander

2 tsps ground cumin

¼ tsp turmeric

½ cup plain yogurt

½ cup water

Salt to taste

1 Tbsp ground almonds

2 green chilies, halved and seeded

2 sprigs fresh coriander, chopped

Fry the onion in the oil until golden brown. Add the cinnamon, cloves, cardamoms, bay leaf, and the cumin seeds. Fry for 1 minute. Add the ginger and garlic paste and the cubed lamb. Sprinkle over the chili powder, ground coriander, cumin, and turmeric and mix together well. Stir in the yogurt, cover the pan and cook over a moderate heat for 10-15 minutes, stirring occasionally. Add the water and salt to taste, re-cover and simmer gently for 30-40 minutes, or until the meat is tender. Just before serving, add the almonds, chilies, and coriander sprigs. Stir in a little more water if necessary, to produce a medium-thick gravy.

Time: Preparation takes about 15 minutes and cooking takes 40-50 minutes.

Freezing: This recipe will freeze well for up to 3 months, but do not add the chilies before freezing, as the process intensifies their heat.

Enchiladas

Sauces and fillings for enchiladas can be infinitely varied to suit individual tastes.

SERVES 6

Tortillas

2 cups all-purpose flour (more if necessary)

2 tsps baking powder

Pinch of salt

4 Tbsps vegetable shortening

½-¾ cup hot water

Oil for frying

Tomato sauce

10 ripe tomatoes, peeled, seeded, and chopped

1 small onion, chopped

1-2 Tbsps tomato paste

1-2 green or red chilies, seeded, and chopped

1 clove garlic, finely chopped

Salt and freshly ground black pepper

Pinch of sugar

2 Tbsps butter or margarine

2 eggs

1 cup heavy cream

Filling

12 oz ground pork

1 small red bell pepper, chopped

4 Tbsps raisins

4 Tbsps pine nuts

Salt and pepper

4 Tbsps shredded cheese

Sliced green onions, to garnish

Sift the flour, baking powder and salt into a bowl. Cut in the shortening until the mixture resembles coarse crumbs. Add water, mixing until absorbed. Knead gently and add more flour if the dough is too sticky. Cover and leave to rest for 15 minutes. Divide the dough into ten even-sized pieces. Roll into balls on a floured surface, cover and leave to stand for 20 minutes. Roll out each ball on a lightly floured surface to a circle 7 inches in diameter. Cover the finished tortillas while rolling all the remaining dough – you should have 12 tortillas in total. Place a lightly oiled skillet over high heat. Fry the tortillas individually on both sides until bubbles form on the surface. Stack them as they are cooked and set them aside until ready to use.

To make the sauce, place tomatoes, onion, tomato paste, chilies, garlic, salt, and sugar in a blender or food processor and purée until smooth. Melt butter or margarine in a large saucepan. Add the paste and simmer for 5 minutes. Beat together the eggs and cream, mixing well. Add a spoonful of the hot tomato paste to the cream and eggs and mix quickly. Return mixture to the saucepan with the rest of the tomato paste. Heat slowly, stirring constantly, until the mixture thickens. Do not boil.

Meanwhile, cook the pork and bell pepper slowly in a large skillet. Use a fork to break up the meat as it cooks. Turn up the heat when the pork is nearly cooked and fry briskly for a few minutes. Add the raisins, pine nuts, and

seasoning. Combine about ¼ of the sauce with the meat and divide mixture evenly among all the tortillas. Spoon on the filling to one side of the center and roll up the tortilla around it, leaving the ends open and some of the filling showing. Place enchiladas seam side down in a baking dish and pour over the remaining sauce, leaving the ends uncovered. Sprinkle over the cheese and bake in a preheated 350°F oven for 15-20 minutes, or until the sauce begins to bubble. Sprinkle with the sliced onions and serve immediately.

Time: Preparation takes 60 minutes and cooking takes about 30 minutes.

Kofta Curry

Koftas are popular throughout India. They are made using lean ground lamb which is blended with herbs and spices.

SERVES 4

Koftas

1 pound lean ground lamb

2 cloves garlic, chopped

1/2-inch cube fresh ginger root, peeled and coarsely chopped

1 small onion, coarsely chopped

1/4 cup water

1 fresh green chili, seeded and chopped

2 Tbsps chopped fresh coriander

1 Tbsp fresh mint leaves, chopped

1 tsp salt or to taste

Sauce

5 Tbsps oil	2/3 cup warm water
2 medium onions, finely chopped	1/2 tsp salt or to taste
1/2-inch cube ginger root, peeled and grated	2 cardamom pods, opened
2 cloves garlic, finely chopped	4 whole cloves
2 tsps ground coriander	2 bay leaves, crumbled
1 1/2 tsps ground cumin	2 Tbsps thick set plain yogurt
1/2 tsp turmeric	2 Tbsps ground almonds
1/4-1/2 tsp chili powder	1 Tbsp chopped fresh coriander
1 small can of tomatoes	
2-inch piece of cinnamon stick, broken up	

Put half the lamb, all the garlic, ginger, onion, and the water into a saucepan and place over medium heat. Stir until the mince is heated through. Cover and simmer until all liquid evaporates (30-35 minutes) then cook, uncovered if necessary, to dry out excess liquid. Combine the cooked lamb with the rest of the ingredients, including the raw lamb. Put the mixture into a food processor or blender and blend until smooth. Chill the mixture for 30 minutes. Divide the mixture into approximately 20 balls, each slightly bigger than a walnut. Rotate each ball between your palms to make neat round koftas. Heat the oil for the sauce over medium heat and fry the onions until they are just soft. Add the ginger and garlic and fry for 1 minute. Add the coriander, cumin, turmeric, and chili powder, and stir quickly. Add one tomato at a time, along with a little juice to the spice mixture, stirring until mixture begins to look dry. Now add the water, salt, cardamom, cloves, cinnamon, and the bay leaves. Stir once and add the koftas. Bring to a boil, cover and simmer for 5 minutes. Beat the yogurt with a fork until smooth, add the ground almonds, beat again, and stir gently into the curry. Cover and simmer until the koftas are firm. Stir the curry gently, cover again, and simmer for a further 10-15 minutes, stirring occasionally to ensure that the thickened sauce does not stick to the pan. Stir in half the fresh coriander and remove from the heat. Sprinkle with the remaining coriander before serving.

Time: Preparation takes about 40 minutes, and cooking takes 1 hour in total.

Sweet Pepper Steaks

In this recipe, peppers, mustard, and capers blend together to make a delicious spicy sauce for steak.

SERVES 4

4 sirloin steaks, approximately 4 oz each in weight

2 cloves garlic, finely chopped

Freshly ground black pepper

4 Tbsps oil

2 shallots, finely chopped

5 Tbsps capers

1 cup sliced mushrooms

2½ Tbsps all-purpose flour

1¼ cups dark broth

5 tsps ready-made mustard

2½ tsps Worcestershire sauce

⅔ cup white wine

2½ tsps lemon juice

Pinch each of dried thyme and rosemary

8 baby corn on the cobs, cut in half lengthwise

1 green bell pepper, finely sliced

1 red bell pepper, finely sliced

1 yellow bell pepper, finely sliced

4 tomatoes, peeled, seeded and cut into thin strips

Lay the steaks on a board and rub both surfaces with the garlic and black pepper. Refrigerate for 30 minutes. Heat the oil in a large skillet and quickly fry the steaks for 1 minute on each side. Remove the steaks from the pan and set aside. Add the shallot, capers, and mushrooms to the oil and meat juices in the skillet. Cook for about 1 minute. Sprinkle the flour over the vegetables and fry gently until it begins to brown. Pour over the broth and stir well, adding the mustard, Worcestershire sauce, wine, lemon juice, thyme, and rosemary, as the sauce thickens. Return the steaks to the sauce mixture along with the corn, peppers, and tomatoes. Simmer for 6-8 minutes, or until the steaks are cooked, but still pink in the center. Serve at once.

Time: Preparation takes about 30 minutes, plus 30 minutes chilling time. Cooking takes 20 minutes.

Preparation: It is important to fry the steaks initially on both sides as this helps to seal in the meats juices.

Salads & Light Meals

Salads and vegetable dishes are fast becoming a favorite of many people. They appeal not only to our growing love affair with healthy foods, but also to our taste for lighter more colorful food. Salads have blossomed from the piece of sad lettuce and tomato that was so familiar just a few years ago, into an area of cooking that is a hotbed of creative and vibrant talent. Salads are no longer the simple mix of light ingredients they once were and today's salads can incorporate everything from fruit and cereals, to pasta, and fish and seafood.

Salads are also no longer served only in the summer, they are popular all year round. As with all vegetable dishes it is best (and most economical) to use vegetables that are in season. Due to modern farming methods a surprisingly large number of vegetables are available throughout the year, but many of these are below par out of their natural season. Obviously, spring and summer are the times when most conventional salad ingredients are at their best, but fall and winter herald the opportunity to be creative with many vegetables we would cook in other circumstances – mushrooms, fennel, cauliflower, and broccoli, for instance, are all delicious raw. Salads which combine vegetables with ingredients such as eggs or pulses, are also perfect as entrées for heartier winter appetites. This chapter features many exciting salad dishes that are perfectly suitable for serving alone – Hot Pepper Egg Salad and Mexican Chicken and Pepper Salad are good examples.

The wonderful combination of colors, textures, and flavors so appealing in salads has also influenced the standard we now expect from cooked vegetable dishes. Add to this the current emphasis on eating more vegetables and you begin to understand why vegetable dishes have become so important. More and more people who are not vegetarians are eating vegetarian meals as a part of their drive towards a healthier diet and this growing trend is bound to increase the demand for top quality vegetable dishes still further. Here, we feature many dishes that are perfect for a vegetarian meal (try Vegetable Curry or Red Bean Stew, for instance), as well as many others, such as Spanish Eggplants and Sri Lankan Rice, that can be served as a snack or as an accompaniment to a meat course.

People who profess not to enjoy vegetable dishes have often been at the receiving end of overcooked, boiled vegetables that would do little for anyone's tastebuds. Not only do today's methods of preparing vegetable dishes avoid this pitfall but these recipes, which further enhance the ingredients with a hot and spicy flavor, add a new dimension to an area of cooking that is finally beginning to gain the popularity it deserves.

Curried Rice Salad

Curry powder, coconut, and mango chutney add an exotic flavor to this rice salad.

SERVES 6

6 oz long grain rice
1 Tbsp curry powder
4 green onions, sliced
2 stalks celery, sliced
1 small green bell pepper, diced
10 black olives, halved and pitted
2 oz golden raisins
2 oz toasted slivered almonds
4 Tbsps shredded coconut
2 hard-cooked eggs, chopped

Dressing
⅔ cup mayonnaise
1 Tbsp mango chutney
Juice and grated rind of ½ lime
4 Tbsps plain yogurt

Garnish
2 avocados, peeled and cubed
Juice of ½ lemon or lime

Cook the rice in boiling salted water for about 15 minutes, or until just tender. During the last 3 minutes of cooking time drain away half the water and stir in the curry powder. Continue cooking over a gentle heat until the rice is just cooked and the water evaporated. Cover and leave to stand for about 5 minutes. Fork through the rice to separate the grains, drain any excess water and set aside to cool. Combine with the remaining salad ingredients, stirring carefully so that the eggs do not break up. Mix the dressing ingredients together thoroughly. Finely chop any large pieces of mango in the chutney. Stir the dressing into the salad and toss gently to coat. Arrange the rice salad in a mound on a serving dish. Sprinkle the cubed avocado with the lemon juice to keep it green and place around the rice salad before serving.

Time: Preparation takes 20 minutes and cooking takes about 15 minutes.

Variation: Use brown rice instead of white and increase cooking time to 30 minutes.

Mexican Chicken & Pepper Salad

A cool lunch for the summer is given character here by the addition of chili, cayenne, and paprika.

SERVES 6

1 pound cooked chicken, cut in strips
½ cup mayonnaise
½ cup plain yogurt
1 tsp chili powder
1 tsp paprika
Pinch of cayenne pepper
½ tsp tomato paste
1 tsp onion paste
1 green bell pepper, finely sliced
1 red bell pepper, finely sliced
6 oz frozen corn, defrosted
6 oz cooked long grain rice, to serve

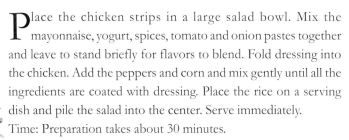

Place the chicken strips in a large salad bowl. Mix the mayonnaise, yogurt, spices, tomato and onion pastes together and leave to stand briefly for flavors to blend. Fold dressing into the chicken. Add the peppers and corn and mix gently until all the ingredients are coated with dressing. Place the rice on a serving dish and pile the salad into the center. Serve immediately.

Time: Preparation takes about 30 minutes.

Spanish Eggplant

This delicious eggplant dish is reminiscent of Spain, where tomatoes, rice, and tuna fish are popular ingredients.

SERVES 4

4 small eggplants
4 Tbsps olive oil
1 small onion, finely chopped
1 clove garlic, finely chopped
¾ cup cooked whole grain rice
7 oz can tuna in oil, drained and fish coarsely flaked
1¼ Tbsps mayonnaise
1¼ tsps curry powder
4 fresh tomatoes, peeled, seeded, and chopped
1 Tbsp coarsely chopped fresh parsley
Freshly ground black pepper

Cut the eggplants in half lengthwise. Score the cut surfaces lightly with a sharp knife at regular intervals. Brush the scored surface lightly with 1 tablespoon of the olive oil and place the eggplants on an oiled baking dish. Bake the eggplants in a preheated 375°F oven for 15 minutes, or until beginning to soften. Cool the eggplants slightly, then carefully scoop the flesh from the center of each half. Take care that you do not break the skin at this stage. Fry the chopped onion gently in the remaining olive oil for 3 minutes, or until it is just transparent. Add the garlic and the eggplant flesh, and fry for another 2 minutes. Season to taste with pepper. Add the rice, flaked tuna, mayonnaise, curry powder, tomatoes, parsley, and black pepper to the eggplant mixture, and mix together well. Pile equal amounts of this rice and tuna filling into the eggplant shells. Return the filled eggplants to the ovenproof baking dish. Brush with the remaining olive oil, and bake in the oven for a further 25 minutes.

Time: Preparation will take 40 minutes and cooking takes about 50 minutes.

Serving Idea: Serve with a mixed leaf salad and black olives.

Hot Pepper Egg Salad

Eggs make the perfect salad, lunch or brunch dish.

SERVES 4

4 eggs
½ bunch of green onions, chopped
½ small red bell pepper, chopped
½ small green bell pepper, chopped
4 oz cooked, peeled shrimp
1 small jar artichoke hearts, drained and quartered
Shredded lettuce, to serve

Dressing
6 Tbsps oil
2 Tbsps white wine vinegar
1 clove garlic, finely chopped
1 tsp dry mustard
1 small fresh chili, seeded and finely chopped
Salt

Prick the large end of the eggs with an egg pricker or a needle, and lower carefully into boiling, salted water. Bring back to a boil, rolling the eggs in the water with a spoon, then cook for 9 minutes. Drain and rinse under cold water until completely cool. Peel and quarter. Combine the eggs with the other salad ingredients in a large bowl. Mix the dressing ingredients together using a whisk to get a thick emulsion. Pour the dressing over the salad and mix carefully so that the eggs do not break up.
Time: Preparation takes about 30 minutes.

Mushroom Curry

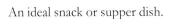

An ideal snack or supper dish.

SERVES 4

1½ cups leeks, finely sliced
2 cloves garlic, finely chopped
½ tsp grated fresh ginger root
2 tsps curry powder
1 tsp garam masala
2 Tbsps oil
6 cups mushrooms, cut into quarters
½ cup grated coconut
1 cup water
1 Tbsp lemon juice

Fry the leeks, garlic, ginger, and spices in the oil until soft. Add the mushrooms and cook over a low heat until soft. Add the grated coconut and half of the water. Cook gently until the coconut has completely softened, adding extra water if the mixture appears too dry. Stir in the lemon juice and sufficient salt to taste. Serve on a bed of rice.
Time: Preparation takes 15 minutes and cooking takes about 20 minutes.
Serving Idea: Serve with a tomato and onion salad.

Gado Gado

Lightly cooked vegetables are enhanced by a delicious peanut sauce in this popular Indonesian recipe.

SERVES 4

1 Tbsp oil

1 carrot, peeled and cut into thin strips

1 potato, peeled and cut into thin strips

4 oz green beans, trimmed

4 oz Chinese cabbage, shredded

4 oz bean sprouts

½ cucumber, cut into thin strips

Peanut sauce

2 Tbsps oil

½ cup raw shelled peanuts

2 red chilies, seeded and finely chopped

2 shallots, finely chopped

1 clove garlic, finely chopped

½ cup water

1 tsp brown sugar

Juice of ½ lemon

½ cup coconut milk

Salt

Garnish

Sliced hard-cooked eggs

Cucumber, sliced or cut into strips

Heat a wok and add 1 tablespoon oil. When hot, add the carrot and the potato. Stir-fry for 2 minutes then add the beans and cabbage. Cook for another 2 minutes, add the bean sprouts and cucumber, and stir-fry for an additional 2 minutes. Place the vegetables in a serving dish.

To make the peanut sauce, add the remaining 2 tablespoons oil to the wok and fry the peanuts for 2-3 minutes. Remove and drain on paper towels. Blend or pound the chilies, shallots, and garlic to a smooth paste. Grind the peanuts to a powder. Heat the wok again and fry the chili paste in the remaining oil for 2 minutes. Add water and bring to a boil. Add the peanuts, brown sugar, lemon juice, and salt. Stir until the sauce is thick – about 10 minutes. Add the coconut milk and stir. Garnish the vegetable dish with sliced hard-cooked egg and the cucumber, and serve with the peanut sauce.

Time: Preparation takes 20 minutes and cooking takes 30 minutes.

Carrot & Coconut Salad

Grated carrots and coconut makes a simple but appetizing salad.

SERVES 4-6

3-4 carrots
2 Tbsps finely grated coconut
2 Tbsps finely shredded onion
1 Tbsp lemon juice
2 Tbsps chopped fresh coriander
1 fresh green chili, seeded and coarsely chopped
½ tsp salt or to taste

Peel and grate the carrots. Combine all the ingredients in a bowl except salt. Stir in the salt just before serving.
Time: Preparation takes 10 minutes.
Variation: Add 1 tablespoon finely chopped fresh mint instead of the coriander.

Spicy Channa Dhal

This is a specialty of the north-eastern region of India.

SERVES 4-6

1 cup channa dhal or yellow split peas
3 Tbsps unsalted butter
1 large onion, finely sliced
2 cinnamon sticks, each 2 inch long, broken up into 2-3 pieces
5 cardamoms, split open on the top
2-4 dried red chilies, coarsely chopped
½ tsp turmeric
½ tsp chili powder
1¼ tsps salt or to taste
2½ cups warm water
2 bay leaves, crumpled
¼ cup flaked coconut
2 ripe tomatoes, skinned and chopped
2 Tbsps chopped fresh coriander

Clean and wash the channa dhal or the yellow split peas and soak them for at least 2 hours. Drain well.

Melt the butter over medium heat and fry the onions, cinnamon, cardamom, and chili peppers for 6-7 minutes, or until the onions are lightly browned. Add the dhal, turmeric, chili powder and salt. Stir-fry the dhal for 2-3 minutes. Adjust heat to low and fry the dhal for a further 3-4 minutes, stirring frequently. Add the water, bay leaves, coconut and tomatoes. Bring to a boil, cover the pan and simmer for 35-40 minutes. Stir in the coriander and remove from the heat.
Time: Preparation takes 5-10 minutes plus time needed to soak the dhal. Cooking takes 50-55 minutes.

Spicy Vegetarian Pizza

This wholesome vegetarian pizza has a very rich flavor.

MAKES ONE 10-INCH PIZZA

10-inch thin-crust pizza base
4 Tbsps olive oil
1 large onion, chopped
2 cloves garlic, finely chopped
1 red chili, seeded and chopped
1 green chili, seeded and chopped
14 oz can chopped tomatoes
Dash of Tabasco (optional)
½ red bell pepper, seeded
½ green bell pepper, seeded
½ yellow bell pepper, seeded
1 cup mushrooms, sliced
Chopped fresh marjoram or ½ tsp dried marjoram
2 oz Cheddar cheese, grated
2 oz Red Leicester cheese, grated

Heat 2 tablespoons of the oil in a saucepan and fry the onion, garlic, and chilies for about 5 minutes or until softened. Stir in the tomatoes and the Tabasco, if using; bring to a boil, then reduce the heat and simmer gently for 15 minutes. Slice 1 or 2 rings from the peppers and set aside. Chop the remaining peppers. Heat the remaining oil in a skillet and fry the chopped peppers for 2 minutes. Add the mushrooms and continue to cook for 3 minutes. Spread the tomato sauce over the pizza base and cover with the sautéed peppers and mushrooms. Mix together the marjoram and cheeses and sprinkle over the pizza. Top with the reserved pepper rings and brush the rings with a little extra oil. Bake in a preheated 400°F oven for 10-15 minutes, or until the base is cooked and golden.

Time: Preparation takes about 10 minutes and cooking takes about 30 minutes.

Variation: Vary the degree of heat of this pizza by adding more or less chilies.

Spicy Oriental Noodles

A most versatile vegetable dish, this goes well with meat or stands alone for a vegetarian main course.

SERVES 4

8 oz Chinese noodles (medium thickness)

5 Tbsps oil

4 carrots, peeled

8 oz broccoli

12 Chinese mushrooms, soaked 30 minutes

1 clove garlic

4 green onions, diagonally sliced

1-2 tsps chili sauce

4 Tbsps soy sauce

4 Tbsps rice wine or dry sherry

2 tsps cornstarch

Cook the noodles in boiling salted water for about 4-5 minutes. Drain well, rinse under hot water to remove starch and drain again. Toss with about 1 tablespoon of the oil to prevent sticking. Using a large, sharp knife or Chinese cleaver, slice the carrots thinly on the diagonal. Cut the flowerets off the stems of the broccoli and divide into even-sized sections. Place the vegetables in boiling water for about 2 minutes to blanch. Drain and rinse under cold water, and leave to drain dry. Remove and discard the mushroom stems and slice the caps thinly. Set aside with the onions. Heat a wok and add the remaining oil with the garlic clove. Leave the garlic in the pan while the oil heats and then remove it. Add the carrots and broccoli and stir-fry about 1 minute. Add the mushrooms and onions and continue to stir-fry, tossing the vegetables in the pan continuously. Combine chili sauce, soy sauce, wine, and cornstarch, mixing well. Pour over the vegetables and cook until the sauce clears. Toss with the noodles and heat them through. Serve immediately.

Time: Preparation takes about 25 minutes and cooking takes about 7-8 minutes.

Serving Idea: Serve as a side dish with chicken, meat or fish, or as an appetizer. May also be served cold as a salad.

Red Bean Stew

If you prefer, use canned kidney beans in this recipe.

SERVES 4

¾ cup dried red kidney beans, soaked overnight

2 Tbsps oil

1 large onion, chopped

1 clove garlic, finely chopped

14 oz can tomatoes

½ tsp dried oregano

½ tsp dried basil

½ tsp soy sauce

3 medium potatoes, peeled and diced

Salt and freshly ground black pepper

Chili sauce

2 Tbsps butter or margarine

1 small clove garlic, finely chopped

1 small onion, grated

⅓ tsp chili powder

1 Tbsp cider vinegar

½ cup bean broth or water

Pinch of salt

1 tsp tomato paste

1 Tbsp chopped fresh coriander

1 tsp plain yogurt

Drain the beans, put into a large pan and cover with water. Boil vigorously for 10-15 minutes, turn down the heat and cook for about an hour until the beans are tender.

Heat the oil and fry the onion and garlic until soft. Add the tomatoes, oregano, basil, and potatoes; cover and cook for 20 minutes, or until the potatoes are softened. Season to taste.

Drain the beans, reserving a little of their liquid, and add the beans to the onion and tomato mixture. Cook gently for 5-10 minutes. In a separate pan, melt the butter or margarine and cook the garlic and onion until soft.

Add the chili powder and cook for a further 1-2 minutes. Add the vinegar, broth, salt, tomato paste, and coriander, and cook for 5 minutes. Remove from the heat and leave to cool slightly before stirring in the yogurt. Serve with the sauce handed round separately.

Time: Preparation takes 20 minutes and cooking takes 1 hour 35 minutes.

Vegetable Curry

A wonderfully tasty curry that freezes well.

SERVES 4

Spices
2 tsps turmeric

1 tsp each of cumin, mustard seed, fenugreek, ground ginger and black peppercorns

4 tsps ground coriander

1/2 tsp chili powder

1 pound onions, finely chopped

4 Tbsps oil

1 1/4 cups evaporated milk

2 Tbsps white wine vinegar

14 oz can tomatoes, processed with their juice

1 Tbsp tomato paste

2 tsps brown sugar

1 tsp vegetable bouillon powder dissolved in a little boiling water

4 cups mixed vegetables (e.g. mushrooms, cauliflower, carrots, potatoes, okra)

Grind all the spices together – this amount will make 3 tablespoons of curry powder. Fry the onions in the oil until golden. Add the ground spices, lower the heat and cook for 3 minutes, stirring all the time. Add the milk and vinegar and stir well. Add the processed tomatoes, tomato paste, sugar and broth. Bring to a boil, cover and simmer very gently for 1 hour. Add the vegetables and cook for about 20 minutes or until tender.

Time: Preparation takes 30 minutes and cooking takes 1 hour 20 minutes.

Sri Lankan Rice

Serve this rice hot as an accompaniment to vegetable curries.

SERVES 8-10

3 Tbsps oil

1 medium onion, finely chopped

2 cloves garlic, finely chopped

1 heaped tsp each of ground cumin, ground coriander and paprika

2 tsps turmeric

1/4 tsp chili or cayenne pepper

2/3 cup Basmati rice, washed and drained

1 1/2 cups skim milk

1 tsp salt

Freshly ground black pepper

1 cup snow peas, trimmed and cut in half

1 1/2 cups mushrooms, sliced

2/3 cup corn

1/2 cup raisins

Heat the oil in a large pan, and gently fry the onion and garlic for 4-5 minutes. Add the cumin, coriander, paprika, turmeric, and chili, and fry for a further 3-4 minutes – do not allow the mixture to burn. Add the rice and mix well with the onions and spices for about 2 minutes. Add the milk and salt and pepper, stir gently and bring to a boil. Cover and simmer until all the liquid is absorbed and the rice is cooked – approximately 15-20 minutes. Steam the snow peas, mushrooms, corn, and raisins, and fold into the rice. Serve immediately.

Time: Preparation takes 15 minutes and cooking takes 25-30 minutes.

Curried Shrimp Salad

Here soup pasta and shrimp are mixed with a curried mayonnaise for the perfect summer salad.

SERVES 4

2 Tbsps olive oil
1 clove garlic, finely chopped
1 small onion, chopped
1 Tbsp curry powder
1 tsp paprika
1 tsp tomato paste
½ cup water
2 slices lemon
Salt and freshly ground black pepper
1 tsp apricot preserves
1¼ cups mayonnaise
1½ cups soup pasta
Juice of ½ a lemon
½ pound cooked shrimp, shelled

Heat the oil and fry the garlic and onion gently until soft, but not colored. Add curry powder and paprika, and cook for 2 minutes. Stir in tomato paste and water. Add lemon slices, and salt and pepper to taste. Cook slowly for 10 minutes, stir in preserves, and bring to a boil, simmering for 2 minutes. Strain mixture and leave to cool. Add mayonnaise.

Meanwhile, cook pasta in boiling, salted water for 10 minutes, or until tender but still firm. Rinse under cold water and drain. Toss pasta in lemon juice, and place in a serving dish. Arrange shrimp on top, and pour over curry sauce. Toss well.
Time: Preparation takes 10 minutes and cooking takes 20 minutes.

China Beach Salad

An unusual, refreshing salad that is named for a stretch of beach near San Francisco.

SERVES 4-6

1 pound cooked, peeled shrimp
1 pound seedless white grapes, halved if large
6 stalks celery, diagonally sliced
4 oz toasted slivered almonds
4 oz canned water chestnuts, sliced or diced
12 oz fresh litchis, peeled
1 small fresh pineapple, peeled, cored, and cut into pieces
1½ cups mayonnaise
1 Tbsp honey
1 Tbsp light soy sauce
2 Tbsps mild curry powder
Juice of half a lime
Chinese cabbage or Belgian endive

Combine the shrimp, grapes, celery, almonds, water chestnuts, and litchis in a large bowl. Add the pineapple pieces to the shrimp and toss to mix.

Break the Chinese cabbage or endive and wash them well. If using Chinese cabbage, shred the leafy part finely, saving the thicker ends of the leaves for other use. Place the Chinese cabbage on salad plates. Mix the remaining dressing ingredients thoroughly. Pile the salad ingredients onto the leaves and spoon over some of the dressing, leaving the ingredients showing. Separate the endive leaves and arrange them whole. Serve remaining dressing separately.
Time: Preparation takes about 30 minutes.

Vegetable Niramish

This curry is delicious, and highly fragrant.

SERVES 4

1 small eggplant

Salt

3 Tbsps oil

1 onion, sliced

1 green chili, seeded and finely chopped

1 tsp cumin seeds

1 large potato, peeled and cut into chunks

4 oz cauliflower flowerets

1 small green bell pepper, sliced

2 small carrots, thickly sliced

1 tsp each ground coriander, turmeric, and chili powder

⅔ cup vegetable broth

1 tsp chopped fresh coriander

Juice of 1 lime

Cut the eggplant into chunks, sprinkle liberally with salt and allow to stand for 30 minutes. Rinse well and drain on paper towels. Heat the oil in a saucepan and fry the onion, green chili, and cumin seeds for 2 minutes. Stir in the potato and fry for 3 minutes. Add the eggplant, cauliflower, pepper, and carrots, and fry for another 3 minutes. Stir in the spices and fry for 1 minute, then add the broth. Cover and simmer gently for 30 minutes until all the vegetables are tender, adding a little more broth if needed. Add the coriander and lime juice and simmer for 2 minutes.
Time: Preparation takes about 20 minutes, plus standing time. Cooking takes about 40 minutes.

Crab Louis

This salad is legendary on Fisherman's Wharf in San Francisco.

SERVES 4

2 large cooked crabs

1 iceberg lettuce

4 large tomatoes

4 hard-cooked eggs

16 black olives

1 cup mayonnaise

4 Tbsps whipping cream

4 Tbsps chili sauce or tomato chutney

½ green bell pepper, finely diced

3 green onions, finely chopped

Salt and freshly ground black pepper

To prepare the crabs, break off the claws and set them aside. Turn the crabs over and press up with thumbs to separate the body from the shell of each. Cut the body into quarters and pick out the white meat. Discard the stomach sac and the lungs. Scrape out the brown meat from the shell to use, if desired. Crack the large claws and legs and remove the meat. Break into shreds, discarding any shell or cartilage. Combine all the meat and set it aside. Shred the lettuce finely, quarter the tomatoes, and chop the eggs. Combine the mayonnaise, cream, chili sauce, green pepper, and green onions and mix well. Arrange the lettuce on serving plates and place the crab meat on top. Spoon some dressing over each serving of crab and sprinkle with the chopped egg. Garnish with tomato wedges and olives and serve the remaining dressings separately.
Time: Preparation takes about 30-40 minutes.

Green Lentils with Ginger — & Spices —

There's certainly no lack of taste in this spicy lentil mix.

SERVES 4

¾ cup green or Continental lentils

Water or broth

2 Tbsps margarine

1 medium onion, finely chopped

1 inch piece fresh ginger root, peeled and grated or finely chopped

1 tsp garam masala

1 tsp cumin seeds

1 tsp coriander seeds, crushed

1 tsp green cardamom pods, seeds removed and crushed

1 medium carrot, diced

14 oz can peeled Italian tomatoes

¾ cup mushrooms, finely chopped

1 Tbsp soy sauce

1 Tbsp cider vinegar

Salt and freshly ground black pepper

Chopped fresh parsley or coriander, to garnish

Wash the lentils thoroughly. Place in a large, heavy-based saucepan, cover with water or broth and bring to a boil. Turn off the heat, cover, and leave to begin to swell. Meanwhile, heat the margarine in a separate saucepan and gently fry the onion, ginger, and spices until they are well combined, softening, and giving off a tempting aroma. Add to the lentils, bring to a boil and start to add the other vegetables, allowing several minutes between each addition, beginning with the carrot followed by the tomatoes and the chopped mushrooms. Stir frequently to prevent sticking and check on liquid quantity regularly, adding more water or stock as necessary. Just before the end of the cooking time – approximately 25 minutes depending on the age of the lentils – add the soy sauce, cider vinegar and salt and pepper. Cook for a few more minutes and serve hot garnished with slices of lemon and freshly chopped parsley or coriander.

Time: Preparation takes about 25 minutes, cooking takes about 45 minutes.

Variation: Black olives can replace the chopped parsley or coriander.

Spiced Potato Bites

In Indian cooking, potatoes are used very imaginatively. Here, boiled potatoes are cut into small pieces, sautéed until they are brown and then flavored with a light sprinkling of spices.

SERVES 6-8

3-4 medium potatoes
4 Tbsps oil
½ Tbsp salt or to taste
¼ tsp garam masala
½ tsp ground cumin
½ tsp ground coriander
½ tsp chili powder

Boil the potatoes in their skins until just cooked, cool thoroughly, peel and dice them into 1-inch cubes. In a wide shallow pan, preferably a non-stick or cast iron skillet, heat the oil over medium heat. It is important to have the right pan otherwise the potatoes will stick. Add the potatoes and spread them evenly around the pan. Brown the potatoes evenly, stirring them occasionally. When the potatoes are brown, sprinkle over the salt, garam masala, cumin, coriander, and the chili powder. Stir gently and mix until the potatoes are fully coated with the spices. Remove from the heat.

Time: Preparation takes 30 minutes to boil the potatoes plus time to cool them, cooking takes 10-12 minutes.

Watchpoint: The potatoes must be allowed to cool thoroughly. Hot or warm potatoes crumble easily and therefore cannot be cut into neat pieces.

Salad with Coconut Dressing

Coconut adds a lovely flavor to lightly cooked vegetables.

SERVES 4

1 pound mixture of the following:
Eggplant, cubed and steamed
Green beans, lightly steamed
Carrots, sliced or cut into strips and steamed
Zucchini, sliced or cubed and steamed
Red or green bell pepper, shredded
Green onions, shredded or sliced
Bean sprouts
Cucumber, peeled, seeded and cubed

Dressing
½ fresh coconut, grated and milk reserved
½ tsp shrimp paste
Juice of ½ lemon
1 clove garlic, finely chopped
1 tsp brown sugar
1 red or green chili, seeded and finely chopped
Salt

Steam the eggplant and carrots for 5 minutes. Steam the beans and zucchini for 2 minutes. Allow the cooked vegetables to cool and combine with the prepared uncooked vegetables. Mix the dressing in a blender or food processor until smooth. Toss the vegetables with the dressing and serve.

Time: Preparation takes 45-50 minutes.

Hungarian Sausage Salad

This salad is really delicious; don't worry about the amount of onion used as Spanish onions are mild and sweet.

SERVES 4-6

8 small potatoes, cooked

½ cup oil

1 pound smoked sausage such as kielbasa or bratwurst

1 large Spanish onion, thinly sliced

2 green bell peppers, sliced

4 tomatoes, quartered

Dressing

3 Tbsps wine vinegar

1 tsp Dijon mustard

1 tsp dill seeds, lightly crushed

1 Tbsp chopped fresh parsley

1 tsp chopped fresh dill

Pinch of hot paprika

Salt

Mix all the dressing ingredients together in a medium-sized bowl. Dice the potatoes while still warm, coat with the dressing and leave to cool. If using kielbasa, boil for 5 minutes. Broil the bratwurst until evenly browned on all sides. Slice the cooked sausage into ½-inch slices and combine with the onion, pepper, and tomatoes. Carefully combine with the potatoes in the dressing. Pile into a large serving dish and allow to stand for 1 hour before serving.

Time: Preparation takes about 20 minutes, and cooking takes 25 minutes. The salad should stand for 1 hour before serving.

Spicy Rice & Beans

Rice and beans are natural partners, especially when spiced with bell pepper, cumin, and coriander. This can be served with warm tortillas and a salad, or as a side dish with enchiladas, meat or poultry.

SERVES 6-8

4 Tbsps oil

2 cups long grain rice

1 onion, finely chopped

1 green bell pepper, chopped

1 tsp each ground cumin and coriander

1-2 tsps Tabasco sauce

Salt

3½ cups broth

1 pound canned red kidney beans, drained and rinsed

1 pound tomatoes, drained and coarsely chopped

Chopped fresh parsley

Heat the oil in a casserole or a large, deep saucepan. Add the rice and cook until just turning opaque. Add the onion, bell pepper, and cumin and coriander. Cook gently for a further 2 minutes. Add the Tabasco, salt, broth and beans, and bring to a boil. Cover and cook about 30 minutes, or until the rice is tender and most of the liquid is absorbed. Remove from the heat and add the tomatoes, stirring them in gently. Leave to stand, covered, for 5 minutes. Fluff up the mixture with a fork and sprinkle with parsley to serve.

Time: Preparation takes about 25 minutes and cooking takes 30 minutes.

Salad Huevos — Rancheros —

Originally a cowboy dish consisting of just eggs, chorizo and green onions, this more sophisticated version is now a popular salad.

SERVES 4

1 large red bell pepper

1 chorizo sausage

4 heads Belgian endive

1 large or 2 small zucchini, cut into matchstick pieces

1 small jicama, cut into matchstick pieces

2-3 green onions, shredded

4 Tbsps pine nuts

4 eggs

1 tsp chopped fresh coriander

Dressing

6 Tbsps oil

2 Tbsps lime juice

Dash of Tabasco sauce

Salt and pinch of sugar

Cut the pepper in half and remove the stems, cores and seeds. Flatten each half with the palm of your hand and brush the skin of the pepper with oil. Place the halves under a preheated broiler and cook until blistered and charred. Remove from the heat and place in a clean towel until cool. Peel off the skins and cut the pepper flesh into thin strips. Set aside.

Bring a pan of water to a boil, add the chorizo and simmer for about 8 minutes until tender. Peel the casing off the chorizo while warm and cut the meat into thin strips. Separate the leaves of the endive and slice or leave whole if small. Bring water to a boil and blanch the zucchini and jicama strips for 1 minute. Rinse under cold water until completely cool and leave to drain. Combine with the endive and green onion. Add the strips of chorizo and set aside. Toast the pine nuts in a moderate oven until golden brown – about 5 minutes. Bring at least 2 inches of water to a boil in a skillet or sauté pan. Turn down the heat to simmering. Break an egg onto a saucer or into a cup. Stir the water to make a whirlpool and then carefully pour the egg into the center, keeping the saucer or cup close to the level of the water. When the water stops swirling and the white begins to set, gently move the egg over to the side and repeat with each remaining egg. Cook the eggs until the whites are completely set, but the yolks are still soft. Remove the eggs from the water with a draining spoon and place them immediately into a bowl of cold water.

Mix the dressing ingredients together and pour half over the vegetables and sausage. Toss to coat. Arrange the mixture on individual plates in the shape of nests. Remove the eggs from the cold water with the draining spoon and hold them over a towel for a few minutes to drain completely. Place one egg in the middle of each nest. Spoon the remaining dressing over each egg, sprinkle over the pine nuts and garnish the yolk with chopped coriander.

Time: Preparation takes about 45 minutes and cooking takes about 15 minutes.

Sichuan Eggplant & Pepper

Authentic Sichuan food is fiery hot. Outside China, restaurants often tone down the taste for Western palates.

SERVES 4

1 large eggplant

2 cloves garlic, finely chopped

1-inch piece fresh ginger root, peeled and shredded

1 onion, cut into 1-inch pieces

1 small green bell pepper, cut into 1-inch pieces

1 small red bell pepper, cut into 1-inch pieces

1 red or green chili, seeded and cut into thin strips

½ cup chicken or vegetable broth

1 tsp sugar

1 tsp vinegar

Salt and freshly ground black pepper

1 tsp cornstarch

1 Tbsp soy sauce

Dash of sesame oil

Oil for cooking

Cut the eggplants in half and score the surface. Sprinkle lightly with salt and leave to drain in a colander or on paper towels for 30 minutes. After 30 minutes, squeeze the eggplant gently to extract any bitter juices and rinse thoroughly under cold water. Pat dry and cut the eggplant into 1-inch cubes. Heat about 3 tablespoons oil in a wok. Add the eggplant and stir-fry for about 4-5 minutes. It may be necessary to add more oil as the eggplant cooks. Remove from the wok and set aside.

Reheat the wok and add 2 tablespoons oil. Add the garlic and ginger and stir-fry for 1 minute. Add the onions and stir-fry for 2 minutes. Add the bell peppers and chili, and stir-fry for 1 minute. Return the eggplant to the wok along with the remaining ingredients. Bring to a boil, stirring constantly, and cook until the sauce thickens and clears. Serve immediately.

Time: Preparation takes about 30 minutes, and cooking takes about 7-8 minutes.

Cook's Tip: Lightly salting the eggplant will help draw out any bitterness.

Serving Idea: Serve as a vegetarian stir-fry dish with plain or fried rice, or serve as a side dish.

Eggplant Bake

Eggplants are wonderfully filling vegetables that absorb flavors well.

SERVES 6

2 large or 3 medium eggplants

2½ tsps salt

⅔ cup malt vinegar

2½ Tbsps oil

2 large onions, sliced into rings

2 green chilies, seeded and finely chopped

2 cups peeled plum tomatoes, chopped

¼ tsp chili powder

1¼ tsps finely chopped garlic

¼ tsp turmeric

8 tomatoes, sliced

1⅓ cups plain yogurt

1¼ tsps freshly ground black pepper

1 cup Cheddar cheese, finely grated

Cut the eggplants into ¼-inch-thick slices. Arrange the slices in a shallow dish and sprinkle with 1½ teaspoons of the salt. Pour over the malt vinegar, cover the dish, and marinate for 30 minutes. Drain the eggplant well, discarding the marinade liquid.

Heat the oil in a skillet and gently fry the onion rings until they are golden brown. Add the chilies, the remaining salt, chopped tomatoes, chili powder, garlic, and turmeric. Mix well and simmer for 5-7 minutes until thick and well blended. Remove the sauce from the heat and cool slightly. Blend to a smooth purée using a blender or food processor.

Arrange half of the eggplant slices in the base of a lightly greased shallow ovenproof dish. Spoon half of the tomato sauce over the eggplant slices. Cover the tomato sauce with the remaining eggplant, and then top this with the remaining tomato sauce and sliced tomatoes. Mix together the yogurt, the freshly ground black pepper, and the Cheddar cheese. Pour this mixture over the tomato slices. Cook the eggplant bake in a preheated 375°F oven for 20-30 minutes, or until the cheese topping bubbles and turns golden brown. Serve hot straight from the oven.

Time: Preparation takes about 30 minutes and cooking takes 40 minutes.

Preparation: Make sure that the eggplants are well drained when they are removed from the marinade. Press them into a colander using the back of your hand, to remove all excess vinegar. Do not rinse the eggplant, as the vinegar gives a tangy flavor to the dish.

Index